POOR STUDENTS, RICH TEACHING

MINDSETS FOR CHANGE

ERIC JENSEN

Solution Tree | Press

555 North Morton Street

Bloomington, IN 47404

800.733.6786 (toll free) / 812.336.7700

FAX: 812.336.7790

email: info@solution-tree.com

solution-tree.com

Visit **go.solution-tree.com/instruction** to download the free reproducibles in this book.

Printed in the United States of America

20 19 18 17 16   6 7 8 9 10

Library of Congress Cataloging-in-Publication Data

Names: Jensen, Eric, 1950 author.

Title: Poor students, rich teaching : mindsets for change / Eric Jensen.

Description: Bloomington, IN : Solution Tree Press, [2016] | Includes
   bibliographical references and index.

Identifiers: LCCN 2015042879 | ISBN 9781936764518 (perfect bound)

Subjects: LCSH: Children with social disabilities--Education--United States.
   | Poor children--Education--United States. | Educational
   equalization--United States.

Classification: LCC LC4091 .J457 2016 | DDC 379.2/60973--dc23 LC record available at http://lccn.
loc.gov/2015042879

Solution Tree

Jeffrey C. Jones, CEO

Edmund M. Ackerman, President

Solution Tree Press

President: Douglas M. Rife

Senior Acquisitions Editor: Amy Rubenstein

Editorial Director: Lesley Bolton

Managing Production Editor: Caroline Weiss

Copy Chief: Sarah Payne-Mills

Proofreader: Ashante K. Thomas

Text and Cover Designer: Abigail Bowen

Acknowledgments

I am indebted to the groundbreaking work of many researchers, the vision and patience of Douglas Rife, and the saintly support of my wife, Diane. I also thank the many high-performing teachers whose work has enriched this project, including LeAnn Nickelsen, Whitney Henderson, Jamie Irish, Leslie Ross, Katie Lyons, Victor Shatalov, and Josalyn Tresvant.

Solution Tree Press would like to thank the following reviewers:

Stacie Emert
Principal
Wheeler Elementary School
Tucson, Arizona

Jacque Wyant
Principal
Sioux City West High School
Sioux City, Iowa

Ellen L. Hall
Principal
Claiborne Fundamental Magnet School
Shreveport, Louisiana

Visit **go.solution-tree.com/instruction** to download
the free reproducibles in this book.

Table of Contents

PART THREE

WHY THE RICH CLASSROOM CLIMATE MINDSET? 107

PART FOUR

WHY THE ENGAGEMENT MINDSET? . . . 145

About the Author

 **Eric Jensen, PhD,** is a former teacher from San Diego, California. Since the early 1990s, he has synthesized brain research and developed practical applications for educators. Jensen is a member of the invitation-only Society for Neuroscience and the President's Club at Salk Institute of Biological Studies. He cofounded SuperCamp, the first and largest brain-compatible academic enrichment program, held in sixteen countries with over sixty-five thousand graduates.

Jensen has authored over twenty-eight books, including *Teaching With Poverty in Mind, Tools for Engagement, Engaging Students With Poverty in Mind, Turnaround Tools for the Teenage Brain, Bringing the Common Core to Life in K–8 Classrooms,* and *Different Brains, Different Learners.*

To learn more about Eric Jensen's teacher workshops and leadership events, visit Jensen Learning (www.jensenlearning.com).

Preface

This brief (and true) story is about a boy whose life took a grim turn for the worse at age two when his mother walked out. After four bizarre years of neglectful caregivers, his dad remarried (for the second of four times). His new stepmother was violent, alcoholic, and abusive. She made the home life a living nightmare for her stepchildren. This boy never—ever—went into the kitchen when she was there, because that's where the knives were. This kid's older sister moved out and lived next door with the neighbors for seven years, and his other sister moved into the garage with no bathroom for eight years.

The boy's father felt trapped in a bad marriage. He worked during the day, went to night school, and had busy weekends with the National Guard. The boy was often locked out of his own house, and he snacked from a bag of dry dog food in the garage in between meals. From second through tenth grades, his violent stepmother terrorized and abused him. To escape the hellish home, his dad sent him to live with his aunt and uncle (a new school), with his grandmother (another new school), or with his sister to live independently (another new school). This boy understood chaos on a daily basis.

After each move away, his stepmother would promise to be good, and they'd move back home. The cycle of violence repeated itself again and again. Moving around was the norm, not the exception; this kid went to three elementary schools, four middle schools, and two high schools. At one count, he had 153 teachers.

The K–12 school experience was disconnected, and the home experience was terror. This kid was never at any school long enough to develop many friendships. He was often truant and sent to the office for discipline issues. In class, he usually sat in the back, stressed and wondering, "What is it going to be like when I get home? Will I get hurt again?" For him, home was a source of chronic stress. Yet, all of this felt absurdly typical. Among his three closest male friends, two also had abusive parents.

Why am I telling you this story? This story is about me, and it is the real story of my early life.

I have been criticized because I write about poverty and I am white and middle class. Guess what? Bad things can happen to people of any religion, socioeconomic class, or ethnicity. I have been told that since I didn't grow up in poverty, maybe I don't know adversity. It is likely you have no idea how I grew up. I have had a loaded, cocked gun held to my head, and I heard, "Do what I tell you, or I *will* shoot!" I was arrested twice, and I barely graduated from high school. Honestly, I do know a little bit about getting knocked down and, more important, about getting back up.

That's what this book is about: choice. Everyone gets knocked down; for some, it is more often and more traumatic than others. But you still have a choice—are you going to get up or not? This book is about how you can give students a helping hand to get up until they can learn to do it for themselves.

You'll hear me say this several times in this book: "Life's not fair, but you *always* have a choice." You have choice in the classes you take at a university, job you interview for, the job you accept, the attitude you bring to work, what you do at work, the people you call friends, the food you eat, the person you marry, the children you have (or don't), how you raise your children, and how you spend your time. Yes, you do have a choice.

The easy way out is to say, "No, I don't have a choice. You wouldn't believe my monthly expenses and how small my paycheck is. You don't know how hard it is just to get by." Actually, I would believe how hard it is to make it. Like many, I have declared bankruptcy, and I've written bad checks just to survive another week or another month. However, once I realized I had a choice, my life changed. I learned to eat on thirteen dollars a month (seriously) just to keep my expenses down (I ate mostly oatmeal and potatoes). I rented and lived in a laundry room for two years ($25 per month) because I couldn't afford rent for an entire bedroom (or to rent an entire apartment). Yes, you do have a choice. Anytime you think you do not have a choice, ask yourself, "If my life depended on doing this, could I change?"

When a gun was held to my head, and I was told, "Do what I tell you, or I *will* shoot," *I called the bluff*. I was young at the time and both stupid and lucky (or I wouldn't be here today). So, I am telling you, even with a gun to my head, I had a choice, and you do too. You *always* have a choice. Because you have choices, you can make this journey in education not just to survive but also to make it the best journey of your life. There is nothing better than knowing that you had a direct impact on helping a student become college or career ready.

Introduction

The title of this book, *Poor Students, Rich Teaching*, suggests it is about succeeding with students from poverty. It is also about something that many poor students are not getting: *rich* teaching. Here, the word *rich* means bountiful. Based on my past, I could have just as easily become a dropout, but several teachers cared about me. They made the rich-teaching difference, and you can too. Every student that you help graduate means one less dropout, which means one less student at risk for getting into the juvenile justice system, receiving welfare, or going to prison. Finally, if you're a teacher who has lost faith in the system, I have a message of hope. You can do this because you always have a choice. I'll show you how to teach differently, and you'll start loving your job again.

I am fully aware that there are other ways that would help solve poverty than what you do in your classroom. I just don't see those other ways happening anytime soon. So, I'm inviting you to do what you can, with what you have, in areas where you have some influence over the outcomes. Ignore the political, social, and economic "noise" out there, and focus on helping each of your students graduate. Nothing moves forward when we complain about what we don't have, how we are undervalued, and how we work with some who poison our school culture. Things only move forward when you focus on the path of success for your students.

Today, I dedicate my time to working with teachers in low-performing schools to help students graduate either job ready or college ready. My advocacy is for teachers like you. I'll do anything to help you grow and succeed. I see teachers as the single most critical factor in helping the United States survive and thrive. I just wish policymakers felt that way too, but that's a topic for another book. We need you to be a tough, gritty teacher who is willing to make hard choices to help your students from poverty succeed.

Digging Into This Book

Poor Students, Rich Teaching is designed to be a starter book for those struggling with teaching students from poverty. Even if you have been successful before, my promise is that through this book, you'll become a richer teacher. It will offer you highly effective and research-driven tools you can use right away.

To change student lives, you will have to change *before* any worthwhile change shows up in your students. You may experience some discomfort when you begin applying tools from this book. However, staying the same will ensure there is no chance to succeed with students from poverty. If your personal level of comfort (staying the same) is more important to you than the success of your students, then teaching may not be your calling. Some dislike change so much that they would rather be miserable (and make others miserable too) than make changes.

I'm not telling you the path of change is easy; I'm telling you that it can be done, and you can do it. To help you on your journey, you'll be getting over twenty chapters packed with effective tools. By the way, I would never tell you that every single page in this book will be mind-blowingly new to you; it won't be. What I will tell is that when you apply what's in this book, you'll be an amazing catalyst for positive change at your school.

In chapter 1, you'll learn what's really going on in the United States regarding poverty. You should know the facts, and I'll spell everything out for you. You'll explore how students from poverty may behave and learn differently. In chapter 2, you'll learn why you are more important than ever. Many books start off by telling teachers what to do differently in their jobs. This book is different. In the first two chapters, you'll learn why the suggestions are not just relevant but also urgent. Please do not change anything you do unless you are sold on the *why* and you buy into the research that supports the change. This is the only way to learn, teach, and grow.

In chapter 2, I'll also introduce the theme for this book—developing the powerful tool for change: mindset. A *mindset* is a way of thinking about something. As Stanford University psychologist Carol Dweck (2008) explains, people (broadly) think about intelligence in two ways: (1) either you have it or you don't, or (2) you can grow and change. In the areas of intelligence and competency, you may have more of a fixed mindset (stuck in place) or a growth mindset (capable of changing). Those with a *fixed mindset* believe intelligence and competency are a rigid unchangeable quality. Those with a *growth mindset* believe that intelligence and competency can develop over time as the brain changes and grows.

This book broadens and deepens the mindset theme to many new areas of student and teacher behaviors that you'll find highly relevant. I've detailed four essential mindsets to reach students in poverty, and the remaining chapters of this book focus on each of them. Each part introduces the mindset and the research, with easy-to-implement and highly effective strategies you can use immediately. Here are the four parts.

- **Part one: The relational mindset**—In chapters 3 through 7, we'll explore the relational mindset and begin to discover why the types of relationships teachers have (or don't have) with students are one of the biggest reasons why students graduate or drop out.

- **Part two: The achievement mindset**—In chapters 8 through 13, you'll learn about powerful success builders with the achievement mindset. Students from poverty can and do love to learn, when you give them the right tools.

- **Part three: The rich classroom climate mindset**—Chapters 14 through 18 offer strategies to create an energetic, high-performing class culture, using the rich classroom climate mindset. You'll learn the secrets that high-performing teachers use to build an amazing classroom climate.

- **Part four: The engagement mindset**—Chapters 19 through 23 dig into student involvement in a new way with the engagement mindset. You'll gain quick, easy, and practical strategies for maintenance and stress, for buy-in, and to build community.

There's much more for you to learn, but these four mindsets and the accompanying strategies will make a world of difference when implemented well. That's my promise. Finally, the epilogue offers a quick read summary of the chapters and offers organized tools for immediate application. In the appendix, you'll find useful resources to support your implementation of the book's tools.

This book will support you in making fresh, smart choices in teaching. As a *throwaway kid*, I was believed to be a disruptive loser who didn't care about learning. Actually, I loved learning; it was school I didn't like. However, those few teachers who treated me well, expected great things, and showed me *how* to be better, well, they got my best effort, attitude, and behaviors. The next time you have a student in your class who is acting out or feeling frustrated about class, remember this: *I* was one of those students, and *I* take it personally when someone does not help a student succeed. I am hoping that you choose to help the student graduate career or college ready. This is a powerful book, packed with real science and real teachers using powerful strategies. It's about doing the hard (and smart) work to help every one of your students that you work with graduate college or job ready. I'm hoping you're on board with that goal.

Now, let's find out what's *really* going on. Before you begin, take a deep breath as you open the door to change. An amazing journey is about to begin.

CHAPTER 1

WHY SHOULD YOU CARE ABOUT POVERTY?

We've all noticed that things are changing in America, and they are changing fast. At one school I was working with, a teacher shared some pretty serious frustrations. As she spoke, her eyes moistened, "You want us to do *this* and *that*, plus you say it might be hard—and it might even take months or years! For starters, do you even know how much we are being asked to do these days? Do you know how little support we get from leadership? How do we even know these things you suggest are possible? And, really, why should we even bother? After all, things will change again in a few years, and there'll be some new flavor of the month that we all have to jump on board with again!" She was nearly in tears, and her pain was obvious.

When teachers tell me, "Our jobs have changed," they're right. When teachers tell me, "Students aren't like they used to be," they're right. When staff tell me, "The whole profession has changed," they're right. Lastly, when teachers like you tell me how frustrating their jobs are, I'm on your side. I've been a teacher. I work with teachers, and I know the profession well.

But let's be honest. *The whole world* is different; so much has changed. Compared to only a couple of generations ago, it's a different world. The concerns that teachers shared with me are real, and they are at the heart of a growing, deepening frustration among teachers nearly everywhere. Let's just say it again, "The world has changed!" Now, let's drill down and learn some of the most relevant changes affecting your classroom when we talk about students from poverty.

What Should You Know About Poverty?

There are three critical characteristics you may want to know about poverty. Each of these has high relevance to you because it affects both your time at work and life away from work.

1. Poverty is far more prevalent than you think, and the devastating effects are accelerating.

2. It affects both you and your students in the classroom (in multiple adverse ways—some that you may have never thought about).

3. Because brains can change, you can reverse the academic effects of poverty and help your students graduate college or career ready. The rest of the book will show you how to make that happen.

Let's begin with understanding poverty in a different way. A common way to think of poverty is simple: at school, you've got students from families that qualify for free and reduced school meals. However, poverty is complicated, not simple. First, it's not a culture (Gorski, 2008).

Saying that someone is from poverty tells us nothing about the family. Is it fragmented or intact, caring or careless? We don't know because on the surface, all poverty means is having a low socioeconomic status, but it does not define the individual. My own definition is less focused on federal standards for annual income. Instead, I focus on the common effects of poverty via an aggregate of risk factors. Here's how I define *poverty* in this book: poverty is a chronic experience resulting from an aggregate of adverse social and economic risk factors.

> **Poverty is a chronic experience resulting from an aggregate of adverse social and economic risk factors.**

Poverty could be urban or rural (most poverty is now rural). Poverty could be generational or the result of multiple adverse incidents (such as job loss, bankruptcy, or a divorce). Experiencing just one risk factor (such as a broken-down car, racism, divorce, unreliable child care, a death in the family, an eviction, poor nutrition, chronic stress, or poor health care) rarely places one in poverty. But multiple risk factors almost ensure one would be in poverty. The poor typically have multiple (three to eight) risk factors in their lives (Pungello et al., 2010).

Next, let's understand the true economic impact of poverty in the United States. Read this closely; you'll want to understand this massive and dramatic change happening right now in our society. You have been told the economy is getting better, but the poor might disagree. In 1964, President Lyndon Johnson initiated the War on Poverty, and over fifty years later, the poor have lost. A commentary from Cato Institute Senior Fellow Michael Tanner (2014) asserts the total monies spent on poverty exceed $16 trillion, and poverty rates still remain high. Percentage-wise, we have about the same number of poor than in 1964. Since 1982, the percentage of married couples (black, white, and Hispanic) who are poor has decreased (ChildStats, 2015). However, in the year 2000, thirty-two million people in the United States were in poverty. By 2009, over forty-three million people in the United States were poor (DeNavas-Walt, Proctor, & Smith, 2011). In fact, each generation is getting worse than the last, not better.

A staggering 1.46 million American families live in extreme poverty, with family members surviving on $2 per day of spendable cash or less (Shaefer & Edin, 2012). The number of Americans receiving government food assistance is now a third of the entire United States, a total of over one hundred million people (U.S. Department of Agriculture, Office of Inspector General, 2013).

The sheer number of students who live in households of poverty have risen from 16 percent in the year 2005 to 22 percent by 2010—a huge 37.5 percent increase (DeNavas-Walt et al., 2011). But by 2011, *one in four* (25 percent) school-age children (fourteen million) lived in a family below the poverty line (Federal Interagency Forum on Child and Family Statistics, 2011).

By early 2015, the majority (51 percent) of all U.S. students in public schools came from homes that met the federal standards for poverty. Texas, California, and Florida all have over 50 percent of their public school students from poverty (Suitts, 2015). If you see more students from poverty in your classroom, school, or district, now you know; it's no illusion. And what's more alarming is that it's getting worse every year.

The United States has orchestrated biased social and economic policies. There are marriage penalties, which occur in the tax system when spouses pay more income tax by filing jointly as a couple than filing as an individual. This is detrimental because when two people are married, resources are pooled and the chances of being poor drop (Rector, 2012). We have "look the other way" institutions (including police departments, judicial systems, and public schools) when it comes to institutionalized racism (U.S. Department of Education Office for Civil Rights, 2014). There are reverse incentives (when a welfare recipient realizes that taking a paying job can actually leave one with less disposable income than when receiving a benefits check). This fosters a dependent lifestyle and discourages upward mobility. We have poor economic policies, which discourage family savings with bank interest rates near zero. There are ineffective health policies that promote free meals at school, which are rarely nutritious (U.S. Department of Agriculture, Food and Nutrition Service, 2013). In sum, to escape poverty in America, one must escape the chains of policymakers too.

Now, what is the relevance for you? Many believe that poverty is a problem for the poor. Actually, it is a problem for everyone. Statistically, it is far more likely that you personally will experience downward mobility (dropping down one socioeconomic class) than upward mobility. If you are middle class, the odds are one in four (25 percent) that you'll be poor within ten years (Pfeffer & Hällsten, 2012; U.S. Department of the Treasury, 2007). If you still think your life could never intersect with the poor, answer this question, "Would you meet the federal guidelines for poverty if you lost your job, your car was wrecked, or you were in the hospital for cancer treatments?" That's it; just three big risk factors, and we are all vulnerable.

Greater poverty means we can predict that future federal and state revenues will decline (decreased tax revenues and greater cost of services such as court systems, corrections, and welfare). At the federal level, less revenue means more money printing (to cover the budget deficits), meaning your retirement dollars become worth less (inflation). At the state level (where balanced budgets are mandated), it means the state will be forced to charge you more for services that used to be affordable or free (which reduces your monthly net income). The greater the number (and percentages) of poor in any country, the greater the loss of untapped creativity, cultural contributions, economic strength, community building, and workforce potential.

I am hoping that you see that having an increasing number of poor people will directly affect your paycheck and lifestyle unless we help the next generation graduate college or career ready. The good news is that quality teaching has a greater effect on student achievement than does the adverse effects of poverty (Hattie, 2009; Wenglinsky, 2002). Now, let's connect the dots: how does poverty influence students in your classroom?

How Does Poverty Affect Your Students?

There are three examples of how the students at your school are likely (but not guaranteed) to be different if they grow up in poverty. These are common, but not universal, differences in people from poverty. You could, of course, show me many, many exceptions, which I am aware of. The first is chronic stress, the second is the presence of cognitive gaps, and the third is less emotional support. Let's begin with the most familiar topic: stress.

Stress

You may recall the word *homeostasis* from high school. Homeostasis is a system property in your body and brain that maintains stability and health. When things go awry, your body wants to revert to a "normal" and healthy state. But exposure to acute and chronic stress often disrupts homeostasis, and we don't go back to a healthy level. Your brain's emotional center, the amygdala, triggers a safety alarm too often (hypervigilance) or not enough (hyporesponsiveness). This means your brain has reset your stress thermostat to a new adjusted stress load, known as allostasis (McEwen, 2000). This new adaptive and draining state fosters ongoing physiological arousal and depletion of resources, often taking the form of anxiety, post-traumatic stress disorder (PTSD), or depression. It is a common part of poor people's lives (Evans & English, 2002).

With allostasis, the poor experience more stressors and more intense stressors than do their middle-income counterparts, and the effects become a nagging drain (Evans & Kim, 2007). As a result, the children of parents living in poverty also significantly experience stress disorders than do their more affluent counterparts (Almeida, Neupert, Banks, & Serido, 2005). Early exposure to chronic stress alters the trajectory of, and impairs the development of brains, creating a devastating, cumulative effect (Coplan et al., 1996).

When exposed to chronic or acute stress, the brain copes by changing and becomes either highly reactive (hypervigilant) or under reactive (learned helplessness), and both are simply coping tools (Knowles, Rabinowich, Ettinger de Cuba, Cutts, & Chilton, 2015). Research on the effects of learned helplessness in school reminds us that the behaviors appear as if students are trying to annoy teachers. That's an illusion (Elliott & Dweck, 1988; Peterson, Maier, & Seligman, 1995). As you read about the classroom symptoms of chronic stress, connect these to prior students. You may have had students who sit inert and rarely participate. These students are neither lazy nor unwilling to engage; you just haven't known how to reach them (so far). You'll learn how to engage them later in this book.

You may have had hypervigilant students who were edgy, impulsive, angry, sometimes profane, and willing to get in your face. Those are well-documented symptoms of chronic stress, not indicators that a student is "bad" or unreachable (Kimble et al., 2014). Later in this book, you'll learn how to get better behaviors that can reset their thermostat.

You may have students who display the common attention-deficit/hyperactivity disorder (ADHD) symptoms (impulsivity, poor memory, and poor reflection or prediction skills). But understanding the poverty point of view is critical; those symptoms are also the *exact same* symptoms of stress disorders. Before you label any of your students, remember that *not* labeling students is a top-twenty factor for student achievement (Hattie, 2009). Chronic stress also impacts cognitive skills. When researchers simulated the effects of money stress on middle-class subjects, the resulting drop in cognitive capacity was the equivalent of thirteen IQ points (Mani, Mullainathan, Shafir, & Zhao, 2013). The good news is that you will learn, later in this book, how you can erase the effects of chronic stress in your classroom.

Cognitive Gaps

Another adverse effect on students from poverty is cognitive gaps. Neurocognitive tests contrasting kindergartners from middle- and lower-class families show three large areas of difference in their brains. They are (1) language, (2) memory, and (3) cognitive control (Noble, Norman, & Farah, 2005). One of the most well-known effects of poverty is a scant vocabulary, with preK exposure just over ten million words by kindergarten versus twenty-five to forty million words for the nonpoor (Hart & Risley, 1995). While you may already know this, the reading scores don't always reflect the real issues among the poor.

Students from poverty are often described as *low students* when, in fact, the *low system* they are in has often missed critical evidence and even more critical interventions. Three commonly underaddressed reading issues for the poor are: (1) poor working memory, (2) weak phonological processing skills, and (3) lack of culturally responsive, grade-level books at home. Let's tie these into the research briefly, and we'll get to those in detail later.

First, working memory is a huge predictor for reading and school success, yet the poor have memory deficits (Tine, 2014). Just improving working memory alone has been shown to boost fluid intelligence and reading scores, so we know it is worth teaching (Jaeggi, Buschkuehl, Jonides, & Perrig, 2008). Additionally, using the *gold standard* in research (randomized control trials), working-memory training significantly boosted performance on untrained memory tasks in children identified as having poor working memory. The gain from the training was significant and lasting (Dunning, Holmes, & Gathercole, 2013).

Secondly, phonological processing deficits are a common issue among the poor (Noble, Wolmetz, Ochs, Farah, & McCandliss, 2006). These students often have confused auditory memory processing resulting in weaker listening skills and inappropriate classroom behaviors. For example, when attempting to read, some students are often unable to process, in real time, the differences between similar-sounding phonemes such as /b/ or /t/. This typically triggers student frustration, difficulty with meaning, lower reading scores, and worries about their own cognitive capacity.

Finally, a lack of books at home (a common issue among the poor) can inhibit reading fluency and motivation. This is critical for both those who speak English and those who are learning it.

Less Emotional Support

Our third adverse effect on students from poverty is a lack of emotional support and social skills (Rosenfeld, Richman, & Bowen, 1998).

Children from poverty are more at risk of having just one parent at home (or none) (McLanahan, 1999). Poverty also raises the odds for children's social maladjustment and behavior problems (Eamon, 2001; McLoyd, 1988). The behavioral issues you see in students are more common among poor in part because of less caregiver role modeling as well as chronic and acute stressors (Garner, 1996). There is a powerful connection between emotion and cognition:

When we educators fail to appreciate the importance of students'
emotions, we fail to appreciate a critical force in students' learning.
One could argue, in fact, that we fail to appreciate the very reason
that students learn at all. (Immordino-Yang & Damasio, 2007, p. 9)

Why are student emotions so critical for you to know about? Some emotions are built in, and others must be learned in one's culture. In your classroom, you might expect a student who you've asked to calm down or be quiet to show compliance or an emotion of empathy, but that has to be learned. An unknowing teacher (would this be you?) might say to a misbehaving student, "Hey, don't give me an attitude!" To which, some students respond with a shrug or an unpredicted response.

What *might* be happening is that the student is showing you the only emotion he or she knows how to show (and it does not fit your model of acceptability). This leads the student to feel annoyed at the teacher and vice versa. Remember, many students simply don't know how to respond to you; no one ever taught them. I constantly got in trouble in school; but for thirteen years, not one teacher ever took me aside and explained what behaviors were appropriate and when I should display them. That was a big mistake. Without positive guidance, I just repeated the same mistakes over and over. Bottom line is that if you don't teach students how to behave, they may not know. It would be like a teacher failing a student on every test and never once telling the student *what* he or she did wrong and, more important, what to do *differently* next time.

The clearest connections with emotions are these: when students feel a connection with their teachers and feel respect and trust, they behave and learn better. Student-teacher relationships have a strong effect on student achievement, which are easily in the top 10 percent of all factors (Hattie, 2009). Relationships between students and teachers are more important to students who don't have a loving parent at home. For comparison, teacher subject-matter knowledge is in the bottom 10 percent of all factors (Hattie, 2009). Students care more about whether their teachers care than what their teachers know.

In the last few paragraphs, I have introduced just a sprinkling of differences between the poor and the nonpoor. My guess is that you could think of other differences you see working with students from poverty. Keep in mind, your students did not choose their parents, their DNA, their neighborhood, or their upbringing. We are the ones who have to adapt in *what* and *how* we teach, or we'll lose a whole generation of students.

You are teaching the next generation that will be taking over the United States soon. There are twenty-six million K–12 students (out of fifty-one million total) from poverty in public schools (Suitts, 2015). This is the next generation. They will either become groundbreaking scientists, better politicians, great teachers, wiser CEOs, and savvy inventors who change the world, or they will drop out, stay in poverty, and drain the economy by consuming services instead of paying taxes. It's your choice; what kind of country do you want to live in? Remember, classroom teachers (you) are the single biggest influencer on student chances for graduation. Each of the upcoming chapters will help you join the thousands of teachers who make miracles happen every day in the classroom.

Can Your Students' Brains Change?

One of the more relevant properties in the human brain when it comes to teaching students is neuroplasticity. This property allows the human brain to make new connections, develop whole new networks, and even remap itself so that more (or less) physical space in the brain is used for a particular task. Anytime you're tempted to think a student is stuck at a certain level of cognitive capacity, remember: your teaching matters so much that, when done right, you can make miraculous progress in your students' brains every day of the school year—if you know how.

But if our brain has that much plasticity then there should be real-world results, right? Actually, remarkable results do happen when the daily experiences of you or your students are changed. In one study, sixty-five children from poverty were adopted at ages four to six. All were pretested for IQ, and 100 percent were at or *lower* than an 86. But adoption changed their experiences, which changed their brains (much like going to a strong school), and after eight years in nonpoor environments, the students were retested. The average gain was fourteen IQ points (Duyme, Dumaret, & Tomkiewicz, 1999). Yes, IQ can change, and better experiences can change it.

But maybe you feel that study just reinforces the role of better parenting, not the power of teachers or schools. That's good critical thinking. To respond to that inquiry, we'd have to keep students with the same parents, in the same homes, and only change teachers or schools. That research has been done. When students stop going to school (having summer breaks or leaving school) IQ drops. When schools are better, attendance is stronger and student IQ scores go up (Ceci & Williams, 1997). But what about your own students? Can every brain be changed? Can every student be helped? Can a teacher actually change the brains of his or her students?

Neuroscience shows evidence of brain changes when reasoning skills are taught. Plus, there are changes in brain activation associated with the practice of high-level cognitive skills (Mackey, Singley, Wendelken, & Bunge, 2015). Even just two hours of cognitive training shows changes in the brain (Hofstetter, Tavor, Moryosef, & Assaf, 2013).

Yes, teachers can and do change brains, so let's explore the research for vocabulary, reading, memory, and mathematics.

When you teach students in brain-based ways (strategies that match the learning protocols for maximizing neuroplasticity), the results can be dramatic. Vocabulary instruction for adolescents shows not only increases in gray matter but that the increased density of gray matter was correlated with higher vocabulary test scores (Lee et al., 2007).

Many teachers struggle with reading but are unsure of how to facilitate the process. When students read for thirty minutes a day for nine consecutive days, a significant amount of new neural connections form (Berns, Blaine, Prietula, & Pye, 2013). Luckily, there are powerful and economical software tools that can help your students build cognitive capacity and erase reading challenges. For example, see Scientific Learning Reading Assistant (www.scilearn.com/products/reading-assistant), a quality neuroscience-based and classroom-tested program (Temple et al., 2003).

The correlation between cortical density increase and the time spent doing mathematics suggests experience-dependent structural plasticity in the brains of those doing mathematics (Aydin et al., 2007). As noted previously, working memory is the silent workhorse of cognition. Working memory is a stronger predictor than even IQ in mathematics (Passolunghi, Mammarella, & Altoe, 2008). In fact, working memory is a greater predictor of all student success at age five than even IQ scores (Alloway & Alloway, 2010). But more important, you can teach working memory in your classroom (Dunning et al., 2013).

Never complain that some students "don't have it." Cognitive skills are teachable, and that fact changes everything about your work. In short, students need better cognitive skills and they are all teachable. They question is, Are you up for changing your students' brains?

Quick Consolidation

This first chapter begins with the "Why we should care." None of us can keep our head in the sand any longer. The numbers of those in poverty in the United States are growing at an alarming rate. Over half of all students in public schools are now on free and reduced lunch. The impact is clear; teachers now have an extraordinary challenge (and opportunity) to alter the course of the United States. How? All of us must find a way to help students graduate college or career ready.

While there are many potential effects of poverty, there are three common ones. First, the poor are more likely to have chronic stressors. Additionally, students from poverty are more likely to have cognitive gaps, increasing the odds for behavioral or social issues. Lastly, many students have less emotional support and have not been taught appropriate emotional response skills. This means, if you don't teach these key life skills, students will likely be punished for things they simply don't understand (as I was as a kid).

Finally, in this chapter, you saw that brains can and do change. Knowing how to do it and having the will to do it are crucial to your success and your students' chances of graduating.

I am hoping that you are sold on the relevancy of learning about poverty. Poverty is reshaping the United States, and you have a big opportunity to make positive changes. If you're ready to get started, good; we need you more than ever.

CHAPTER 2

WHY SHOULD YOU EMBRACE CHANGE?

Education in America is in a dramatic flux state. It seems like half the schools are similar to schools in the mid-19th century and the other half are changing at light speed. Job descriptions for, and demands on, school staff (teacher, teacher aide, principal, and so on) are also dramatically changing. Teachers are expected to learn new curricula, change assessments, and implement new instructional strategies seemingly at the drop of a hat. Financially, many have had benefits and pay increases cut while tenured teachers are less common, and there are now court cases over whether the law protects teacher retirements.

Excuses are not tolerated, and your test scores are often public record. Many unprepared principals are expected to become instant instructional leaders. When U.S. schools, districts, and states get overwhelmed, they can ask for a flexibility waiver that relaxes standards from the government. Unsurprisingly, over 90 percent of all states have already submitted and received some type of Elementary and Secondary Education Act (ESEA) flexibility waiver (Polikoff, McEachin, Wrabel, & Duque, 2013). These are typically a renewable exemption from ESEA requirements (plus the related regulatory, administrative, and reporting requirements). These waivers are granted directly to the districts requesting relief when requirements aren't met. Meeting the No Child Left Behind and Common Core demands has not been easy for many schools.

You may hear unfavorable press about teachers ("Test scores are low!" "Teachers object to new standards!" "Teacher contract talks have stalled!"). If you read and listened to all the negative noise, it could get pretty frustrating and depressing. Stop watching the bad news on TV, and stop listening to others who are circulating negativity. Your work is important, but there will always be critics. Let's focus on ensuring students graduate either job or college ready.

Getting teachers to become more effective is only one solution (of many) to the poverty challenge. But it's a strong one and the one you have some control over. If I had a choice, I would wave a wand to double the salary of 90 percent of all teachers. I would help the lowest performing 10 percent of teachers find another job. Remember, you always have a choice. If you don't like working with students from poverty, consider teaching at a school with middle-class students. Thousands of U.S. schools have staffing shortages. Every student deserves an ally to help him or her graduate. The thinking that will help you succeed is, "I work to help every student graduate job or college ready."

Why You Are More Important Than Ever

If you're in the middle class and think that poverty is someone else's problem, you're wrong. In the U.S. economy, everyone is either a *net taker* (getting welfare, free or reduced school lunch, or social services; serving in the criminal justice system; or so on) or a *net giver* (paying more taxes than the value of the services you consume every year). We all can erase the academic effects of poverty in our own lifetime, but students need your help desperately. You can help them without working one extra hour in the classroom. Here's why you're so important.

- The classroom teacher is still the single most significant contributor to student achievement; the effect is greater than that of parents, peers, entire schools, or poverty (Hanushek, 2005; Haycock, 1998; Rivkin, Hanushek, & Kain, 2005; Rockoff, 2004).

- Research shows that above-average teachers (those who get one and a half years or more of student gains per school versus one year) based on year-on-year progress can completely erase the academic effects of poverty in five years (Hanushek, 2005). Regardless of what you think about the evaluation and measurement of teachers, I think you can recall from your K–12 experience that your own teachers varied quite a bit in effectiveness, as do your colleagues today.

The days of old-school teaching, no accountability, job security, and middle-class populations are over. Everyone's looked at more carefully, and everyone's expected to learn, grow, and change every single school year. Many veteran teachers feel like they're in another world compared to when they started. If you feel the changes you're right on target, but the changes are just getting warmed up. This book is all about another powerful change that soon all teachers are expected to embrace: better mindsets.

The Real Power of Change: Mindsets for Success in Teaching

Every profession requires a host of mindsets for success. For example, in sports, if you think your opposition will win, you're in for a tough game (and probably a loss). You have to believe you can beat any team on any given day. At your job, we've all seen administrators being replaced at school, superintendents at the district level, and policy-makers at the state and federal levels. Every few years, the curriculum we teach changes, and change will continue to happen. However, one thing must remain stable: you still have the power to block out the noise, and focus on what matters most—helping students graduate. Simply coping in your profession requires a strong mindset. But to thrive? That's what this book is all about.

In teaching, you *have to believe* that every single student (100 percent of your students with no exceptions) can improve a great deal and that you're willing and able to make it happen. You *have to believe* that you are the biggest difference maker in each student's life. You *have to believe* that no matter what else is going on in that learner's life, once class starts, you can make the magic happen. You *have to believe* you can connect, inspire, and energize every student. If there's just one molecule of doubt in your mind, students will sniff it out and lose faith because they know you don't have faith in them either.

Examining old mindsets and sculpting new ones might be the toughest thing you've ever done. Any teacher can pick up a new strategy and try it out in his or her classroom. That's not a mindset change. We've all done that (countless times), but if that were all it took, the United States would have stratospherically high graduation rates. After all, you have access to the Internet and could download a hundred strategies a day. Clearly, it takes more than the next big thing. We will begin here with something far deeper than another quick fix: a purposeful transformation from less to more effective classroom mindsets. The fresh, nuanced mindsets are:

- **The relational mindset**—Why the types of relationships you have (or don't have) with students are one of the biggest reasons that students graduate (or drop out)

- **The achievement mindset**—Why your attitude about success will make or break students from poverty

- **The rich classroom climate mindset**—Why a rich, energetic, high-performing class culture will transform your teaching and student responses

- **The engagement mindset**—Why engaging students will change their mindsets about participation, learning, and success

Remember, a *mindset* is a way of thinking about something. If you have a fixed mindset, you think failures are generally bad and they make you look less competent or even flawed. Consequently, you'll take *fewer* risks and *avoid* failures at all costs to look good. In contrast, a growth mindset encourages you to think failures are a normal part of the learning curve; so, the only way to succeed is to fail along the way. You learn to embrace failures as long as you keep getting better. Just how good would you be at your job if you got just 1 percent better every week of your career?

If you think all of the changes going on in your profession are disruptive, then you'll likely be pretty stressed. However, if you embrace change as a normal, energizing opportunity to grow, then you'll likely stay excited and psyched up. So how will you deal with this changed and changing world? When you fail, what's your response to it? Given that change is the norm, that change is accelerating and is absolutely required to survive as a strong teacher, is this profession still for you? If change is the new constant, are you changing or falling behind?

Changing your mindset is an opportunity to hold up a mirror and closely examine the thinking (beliefs and attitudes) that makes you who you are. See figure 2.1.

You Are Your Mindset: Which Is Yours?

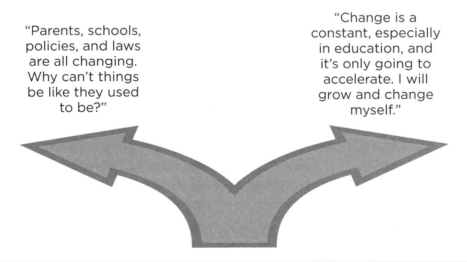

"Parents, schools, policies, and laws are all changing. Why can't things be like they used to be?"

"Change is a constant, especially in education, and it's only going to accelerate. I will grow and change myself."

Figure 2.1: You are your mindset—preparing to change your mindset.

Even if you use the highly effective and research-based strategies in this book, it will still take a growth mindset to help yourself (and your students) have the best year ever.

Now, let's add one more element to your improved mindset: research. You (and most other educators) have heard *research based* applied to so many things that it can become meaningless. It's time for you to make it real. Being research based can actually save you time and still give you a greater effect on student achievement.

More-Effective Interventions

In the game of basketball or football, the team that scores the most points wins. The scoring system is simple and universal. In education, the *scoring system* that decides which classroom strategy is a winning strategy is the *effect size*, which is a standardized measure of the relative size of the gain (or loss) of an intervention as measured toward student achievement (Olejnik & Algina, 2000). To understand the value of any education intervention or strategy, research scientists measure the difference between doing something and doing nothing. Ideally, you would have the experimental group and a control group and have large sample sizes and dozens or even thousands of studies (often on a single topic) and possible interventions. Then, you know your data are very, very solid.

But before your eyes glaze over and you're tempted to fast-forward to the classroom strategies you can use, lean in, and read closely. What if, by just switching one strategy (one that you already use, such as saying "Good job") with another strategy that takes the same amount of time, could give you five to ten times the positive effect on student achievement? Now, think about that for a moment. What if you slowly replaced much of what you did (that was "sort of" effective) with strategies that are highly effective? Wouldn't that make your work much more satisfying? Would you embrace the change or stick with the same old path, getting the same results? Simply put, effect sizes are a common research-based way to measure and evaluate the efficacy of any education strategy or factor. While an intervention can, and occasionally does, have a negative effect size, most are positive. They typically fall between 0.25 and 0.75 with the mean about 0.40 (Hattie, 2009). This means that effect sizes above 0.40 are good, and the higher the better. See table 2.1.

Table 2.1: Effect Sizes

Effect Size	Characteristic
0.00 or less	Negative effect
0.00 to 0.20	Negligible, unclear effects
0.21 to 0.40	Small to moderate effects
0.41 to 0.60	Moderate to strong effects
0.61 to 2.00	Extreme positive effects

Source: Coe, 2002.

Throughout this book, I refer to strategies and factors, and you'll often get their effect sizes. To provide a classroom context for these numbers, a 0.50 effect size is one year's worth of academic gains. Effect sizes of 1.0 are two years' worth of gains, and 1.50 equals three years' worth of gains. Therefore, if everything you did (as most teachers do) over a single calendar school year, averaged a 0.50 effect size, you would advance students with one year of academic gains.

However, students from poverty often start school one to three years behind. To ensure they graduate, you'll want to teach in ways that give them one and a half years' worth of gains (or more) in each school year. Remember, without this effect-size increase in your teaching, many students of poverty will never reach grade level and will likely drop out. When students drop out, the country changes and your retirement becomes more at risk. The strategies you will be reading about are not add-ons. They are clear replacements for things you already do (that may be less effective).

This book combines two powerful forces: mindsets and high effect sizes. The broad issue in this book is not about the next big thing. It's about the way you think, your attitudes, and your beliefs as game-changing difference-makers in the classroom. Once you have the right mindset, you'll become an unstoppable force for good, and building student achievement will become natural to you, especially when you start switching out average strategies for better, proven ones with skyrocketing effect sizes.

Yes, it's clear that economic, educational, and social trends do not look promising. The trend is not our friend. But we have to look within for solutions. Failure is unacceptable. Please do not expect big government, state superintendents, governors, or even local school districts to fix student achievement issues. Their track records are rarely inspiring. Focus on where *you* have the most influence. As educators, we must ask ourselves, "What role can I play in the success of struggling students?" The truth is, you can do a lot. Now, I ask you again: Can you, and will you help?

Quick Consolidation

This chapter and chapter 1 reminded you *why* you do your job. When you help students from poverty succeed, it changes the course of the United States. Yes, the politics of educational policy are often ridiculous, and you're likely underpaid and overworked. However, please remember to keep your focus on how to make your student's day.

Shift your mindsets enough to become a seriously powerful change agent and an unstoppable playmaker who makes miraculous events happen every day. If you are on board, the rest of this book will help you get there. If you want to stay in the profession, then embrace it. Never wish you were doing something else. Get busy getting better, or get out. Yes, we all do need to do things differently, so let's embrace the opportunity;

make it a goal for students to like your class so much that they want to come early, stay late, and thank you at the end of class. If that sounds good to you, keep reading; this book is going to support you to get better every chapter.

PART ONE

WHY THE RELATIONAL MINDSET?

CHAPTER 3

SECRETS OF THE RELATIONAL MINDSET

When I first began teaching, I was so excited and wanted to share all my new creative activities, class content, and cool examples that I had generated. I was using demonstrations, reciprocal teaching (students teaching each other), and high-quality feedback. My students loved it. Truth is, I was pretty engaging, and my students' test scores were high. However, I should qualify my success by saying most of my students were like me: white and middle class. This commonality just made teaching easier. It also let me get away with some sloppy teaching too.

As soon as my students were different than me, everything else changed in a big way. My new teacher colleagues alerted me that I had better build relationships with my students before they would listen or even care about the class content. Unfortunately, I was *terrible* at building relationships. It's funny: people tell you to build relationships as if everyone automatically knows how to do it. Honestly, I had no clue.

As a child, I never had good role models who showed me how to build relationships. My mother left when I was two. After that, as you've already read, I experienced manipulative and dysfunctional relationships at home. At school, teachers didn't want to teach me how to behave. They simply told me to behave differently. I was truant often and was in the principal's office for discipline issues. I simply never saw, until I was almost thirty years old, anyone who was in, or ever had, a good relationship. If you're not great at building good relationships, or you are unsure how important they are, this mindset is for you.

The Relational Mindset

In this chapter, we begin with building the narrative of relationships as the core underpinning of high-performance teaching with students from poverty. That means if you're not connecting by giving respect, listening, and showing empathy, you risk losing your students. When students lose interest in school, they will most likely find somewhere else to invest their energy, and their choices may not be good. Some will get their respect and connections through peers and sports, others though drugs or even gangs. All of us are in this together. When your students succeed, you succeed. When they graduate, you succeed. When they get a job or go to college, you succeed. There is no *us* (teachers) and *them* (students). That erroneous narrative (of separation) will ruin your chances of success in teaching. The relational mindset says, "We are all connected in this life together. Always connect first as a person (and an ally) and then as a teacher second."

> The relational mindset says, "We are all connected in this life together. Always connect first as a person (and an ally) and then as a teacher second."

However, I am not telling you that it is impossible to succeed with *every student* unless each likes or respects you. Some students (those from strong, intact families) come from such stability at home that they need *less* relationship time at school. When a student has an emotionally stable family, good friends, and positive relatives, the need for relational stability at school is less. Those students get their need for relationships with their existing family and peers and with participation in arts, sports, or the community. However, those students are increasingly becoming the exception. Regardless of what your students do or say, they need to connect. The more you think you are separate from your students, the worse the relationships. The more students feel separate from you, the greater the problems you'll have with them and the greater the likelihood they'll achieve less. Your students will care about academics as soon as you care about them. As neuroscience tells us, we are hardwired to connect.

Teachers who struggle with relationships may find that the following comments characterize their thinking.

- "I wasn't hired to be their parent; I was hired for the content I know."
- "I'm just not one of those touchy-feely teachers who does the warm fuzzies."
- "I don't even have enough time to do the content as it is, much less add more stuff."
- "If the parents don't care enough to raise them right, how is that my job?"

- "I know their names; what else do you want? I've got enough problems of my own without adding the student problems."

If you have ever heard another teacher voice any of these statements, now you know the mindset of the teacher who may struggle. The relational mindset is the opposite. The relational mindset in the classroom is your way of assuring students that we are all connected in this life together. Teachers with the relational mindset ask:

- "How can I show my students that I care about their home life as well as their classroom successes?"
- "How do I connect first as a person (and ally) and as a teacher second?"
- "How do I put students first, and everything else second?"

When you strive to answer these questions, everything will change for the better, and that's a promise.

A Hard Look at the Evidence

The Commission on Children at Risk (2003), a panel of thirty-three doctors, research scientists, and mental health and youth service professionals, concludes that the need to connect is hardwired. When students feel more connected, they stay in school, achieve more, and are more likely to graduate. Commonly, the high-performing teachers (those with more than one and a half years of annual gains) demonstrate to their class, over and over, that we are all connected and need each other. Separation is an illusion; we are mathematically connected to anyone within just six relationships (Todd & Anderson, 2009). See figure 3.1.

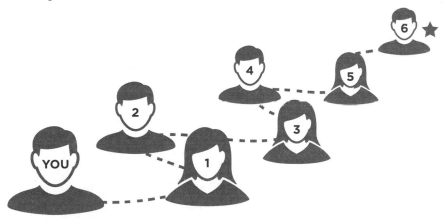

Figure 3.1: Six degrees of separation.

As infants, we need to connect so critically with another human (for food, safety, clothes, shelter, and interaction) that we'll bond with nearly any caregiver, regardless of quality (Moriceau & Sullivan, 2005). Students also want their teachers (that's you) to do more inclusion to integrate their personal experiences into the lessons and facilitate more interactive discussions and team-building activities (Chung-Do et al., 2013). The research tells us that relationships mean more to students who have instability at home than to students who have a stable, two-parent foundation (Allen, McElhaney, Kuperminc, & Jodl, 2004). Interested in higher scores? Evidence shows you that emotional support is that important.

Effective teacher-student relationships contribute to student achievement, and this contribution varies depending on students' socioeconomic status and grade level. Among all students, good relationships have a 0.72 effect size, which makes them an exceptionally significant and strong effect size catalyst (Hattie, 2009). Among secondary students, the effect size is a large 0.87 (Marzano, 2003).

Among elementary students, more so for boys than girls, kindergarten teachers' relationships were significantly correlated with academic outcomes through middle school. In fact, teacher-student relationships are a significant predictor of student achievement even when prior levels of relationships and academic ability are taken into account (Hamre & Pianta, 2001). In addressing relationships with students from poverty, remember that a good adult relationship significantly destresses the student (Miller-Lewis et al., 2014). When students are less stressed, you get better behaviors, better cognition, and more emotional flexibility.

When teachers offer strong instructional and emotional support, students from low-income families *perform equal* to their higher-income peers (Hamre & Pianta, 2005). In fact, by the end of first grade, those so-called at-risk students are learning, have achievement scores, and are behaving like their nonpoor peers. By contrast, students in poverty in less supportive classrooms have lower achievement and more conflict with teachers (Hamre & Pianta, 2005).

In fact, at every grade level, students who feel affinity for the teacher tend to engage more. This is especially true at the secondary level where students often experience feeling disconnected (Pianta, Hamre, & Allen, 2012). And, when researchers look over a period of years, students with highly supportive teachers with low levels of conflict obtain *higher scores* on measures of academics and behavioral adjustment than do students whose relationships with teachers are poor (Hamre & Pianta, 2006).

As you might guess, the effect size on student achievement from effective relationships is stronger for behaviorally and academically higher-risk students and for minorities than for low-risk learners (Hughes, Luo, Kwok, & Loyd, 2008; Liew, Chen, & Hughes, 2010). In the classroom, relationships influence engagement in multiple ways.

First, quality interactions within a relationship provide instruction, correction, modeling, and support for students, forming the basis of a teacher-student relationship (Hughes

& Kwok, 2006). Second, a positive teacher-student relationship enhances students' sense of classroom security and increases their willingness to engage in the classroom (Baumeister & Leary, 1995). Third, evidence shows that quality relationships can help students achieve more through greater connected engagement (Roorda, Koomen, Spilt, & Oort, 2011). Another study reveals that students' positive or negative classroom relationships *are equal to* IQ or school achievement test scores in predicting if a student will drop out (Jimerson, Egeland, Sroufe, & Carlson, 2000).

Reread that last sentence. If you really want to keep students in school, build relationships! Daily, ask yourself powerful questions such as, "When other teachers successfully build quality relationships, how do they do it?" "In what ways can I connect with students that will make a difference for them?" and "How can I help students feel more safe, respected, and connected?"

Relationship building is a critical factor with students from families who have typical poverty risk factors (scarcity of resources, poor medical care, neglect, eviction, less quality time with caregivers, poor nutrition, transportation issues, and so on). Strong relationships can immediately make a positive impact.

In the upcoming chapters, you'll see how relationships offer the emotional environment through which all course content flows. There is no classroom content without some sort of context, even if the context is a digital device. The following three chapters offer strategies to get your students more on board emotionally and socially. These strategies are:

1. Personalize the learning.
2. Connect everyone for success.
3. Show empathy.

Quick Consolidation

When students feel connected, respected, and trusted by their teachers, they behave and learn better, as student-teacher relationships have a strong effect on student achievement.

Relationships between students and teachers are more important to students who don't have a loving parent at home. For comparison, teachers' subject-matter knowledge is in the bottom 10 percent of all factors (Hattie, 2009). Students care more about whether their teachers care, than what their teachers know. If you feel ready to charge ahead and change your classroom, you are about to get powerful strategies you can use immediately.

CHAPTER 4

PERSONALIZE THE LEARNING

In a large noisy crowd, what's the one word (besides "Fire!") that gets your attention? It's your own name. We perk up and listen when we hear our name because we have been conditioned, over a lifetime, to respond to something directed to us and at us. Personalization in your classroom works because our brain cares about itself (Eichenlaub, Ruby, & Morlet, 2012).

This chapter is all about creating a culture of personalization. It's about connecting in a personal way so that your teaching gets students to perk up and pay attention to that which is relevant: themselves. Let's begin with the first of four powerful personalization tools: a name. Then, you'll learn about a Me Bag and how and why to share your own stories through problems and goals. This is a powerful chapter; as you read it, reflect on what you already do. Maybe it will also inspire you to add something new.

Learn Students' Names

To create a culture of personalization starting on day one, learn every student's name. You don't need to be a memory champ to do this. You just need to care and take the time to set up the learning process, then practice, just like the students in your class. When you use a student's name, be sure to smile and make eye contact. Many times, a simple handshake or other appropriate connection will show a lot to your students (you care). You may already be great at learning student names; if not, here are several strategies for you.

Name-Learning Strategies for Teachers

There are many smart ways to remember names and faces. First, put your brain in a curious state. Say to yourself, "OK, what is this student's name? Is it _____?" That primes the brain to care and to listen better. Then, when you hear the name, repetition works, so use it! Also, use it under different circumstances such as standing, sitting, when giving a compliment, or standing at the door. Here are a few strategies for learning names.

- **Introductions:** At the start of the school year, have students say their first names every time they speak. Do this for the first thirty class days (if you have thirty students, or twenty days if you have twenty students).

- **Desk nametags:** Have students create desk nametags from single index cards or cardstock (fold the paper in half horizontally). Have a box for each class of nametags and ask students to pick them up and return them to the box each period. The hard (but good) part is after two weeks, you pick out each name and try to place it on the right student's desk.

- **Checks:** When students are writing, ask yourself quietly, "What's his or her name?" Try to answer it first, then walk over, and check out your answer by looking at the student's name on a paper or asking.

- **Alliteration:** Link a word that begins with the same consonant as the student's first name. Use connections like, "Laura longhair," "Benny in a bowtie," "Michael has a motorcycle," and "Jasmine likes jam." Then, visualize the connection in your mind's eye.

- **Self quizzes:** As students enter the class, greet them by name, or ask them to give you a prompt or cue to trigger their name. Tell students they can't enter your classroom until you say their names correctly. Then, use their names as you make eye contact and give a compliment. ("Eric, good to see you today.")

- **Likes:** Do a quick energizer asking students to stand in areas of the room by likes or dislikes. ("If you like green vegetables, stand over there. Stand over here if you are a St. Louis Cardinals fan.") The point of this activity is to help you remember students by associating them with their preferences.

- **Nametags:** For the first two weeks or so have students wear nametags. Make a contest to see who can learn the most names in class. For younger students, tags will last longer on their backs.

- **Rhyming:** Link a word that sounds like the student's first name to each student. ("Jamal at the mall," "Tim is slim," or "Jake swims in a lake.")

- **"I'm going shopping" game:** Students stand up, one by one. The game begins like this: "My name is Eric, and I am buying medicine for my earache." The next student stands and says, "His name is Eric, and he is buying medicine for his earache. My name is Kim, and I am buying a coke." Each student stands, repeats prior students' statements, and adds his or her own shopping item. You can be the last person to add to the shopping list.

- **Returns:** When you return papers or assignments in the first three to four weeks, use names as you give the paper back to the student ("Loved your perfect spelling, Kenisha").

- **Interviews:** Give students two to three minutes in pairs to interview each other and discover something that no one can forget. Each pair stands, then asks students to introduce each other, allowing about one minute per pair.

- **Classroom roles:** Students apply for (or are given jobs) so you can tie the student to his or her class job ("Ryan the reporter" or "Kayla the class leader").

Name-Learning Strategies for Students

A fun activity for students to learn each other's names is the name game. On a 3" x 5" note card, ask everyone to write one word that begins with the same first letter as his or her first name. The word should connect with something about him or her ("Eric is energetic"). Then, put your students in small groups of four to six. In a circle, ask everyone to say his or her name, the word, and the connection to the word. Then, the group can put the cards in the center of the circle in a box or basket. Using a timer, ask a pair of volunteers to see how long it will take them to return the correct card to the other students in the group. Next week, switch up students so all of them are in a new group. Continue this for the first four weeks until everyone is pretty good at others' names.

These memory tools will build the confidence and social glue to foster cognitive capacity (for attention, short-, and long-term memory). Additionally, during group work, invite students to always address each other by name. When students pair up with a new partner, ask them to introduce themselves to others with eye contact, a greeting, and a handshake. If this seems like a silly practice, I assure you it's not. Strong social glue builds valuable respect, familiarity, and trust. Activities like these break down barriers and reduce cliques in class.

Create a Me Bag

Another way to build a culture of personalization is to use variations of the Me Bag activity during the first week of school. First, you'll model the process for your own students. Start with a paper bag that has small objects, items you collect about yourself: photos, receipts, ticket stubs, a favorite snack, keys, or mementos that are important to you and help tell a story about yourself.

Share those objects and stories in about seven to ten minutes. This is a great activity for all K–12 students. Most students want to know some personal things about their teacher. If you teach at the secondary level, and you think it's still a bit weird, brainstorm with colleagues to come up with alternatives. For example, you might ask students to share using Padlet, Corkboard Me, or Popplet or even PowerPoint.

The Me Bag activity breaks down walls, especially with teens who think, "No one understands me except my friends." When adolescents find out that others have had a pretty rough life, they soften and barriers come down. Share something good, bad, and maybe silly (or embarrassing) that happened to you.

Leslie Ross (2012), a secondary teacher at a high-poverty school in Greensboro, North Carolina, defies tradition and uses the Me Bag activity with all her ninth-grade students (versus using it for only lower elementary). She typically gets among the highest test scores in the district. This teacher says that middle and high school students can get pretty "clique-ish" and stick with their friends too much.

Be real; students need and appreciate your honesty and genuineness. My own Me Bag that I would use if I was back with my own students would have photos of my mother, wife, dad, uncle, and friends; my keys; favorite snack food (nuts); a copy of my diploma; and a pair of swim fins (I enjoy the water).

Share an Everyday Problem

In the preface of this book, I shared my own early life story. I didn't want sympathy or blame; the story is just a part of my early life. I am often hesitant to share it because I am afraid of how it will be received. Will I be thought of as a jerk or someone looking for attention? I don't know. But I do know that when I talk about poverty, it seems to allow others permission to share their story too. And that makes it worth sharing. The third of four powerful personalization tools is your story.

Whether you want to be a role model or not, you *are* a role model. Give students what they need so badly—a real-world model of how to live as an adult. That means about once a week, share a piece of your world. A short, three-minute slice of a teacher's life can do wonders for the relational mindset. Consider the following teacher's story.

"Last weekend something weird happened. I had promised to help my friend move on Saturday. But when I went out to my car that morning, I turned the key to start it and *click* . . . nothing! My car wouldn't start, and I was freaking out because I made a promise to her. 'Friends keep promises to friends,' I said to myself. Now, what could I possibly do?

"Well, students, it's time for your challenge of the day. Work with a partner, and come up with two possible solutions to my problem. You see, even though I was freaking out, I found a way to solve the problem. How would you solve this problem?"

The solution is less important than the process. First, your story gives students a tiny window into your adult world. Second, you turn it into a learning opportunity for them to learn to solve real-world problems. After a minute for student brainstorming, call on students, and don't judge their answers. Keep a modest, positive spirit, and say, "I hadn't thought of that. Thank you, Marcus" or "I appreciate the brainstorming you guys did. Thank you. Now, let's grab a few more ideas." I always thank them but never criticize, judge, or evaluate their efforts. I realize they're a fraction of my age and are unlikely to have the same coping skills. Thank them for taking the risk to jump in.

By the way, their answers are likely to be inappropriate. After you call on many volunteers (thanking them for their effort), you should share the rest of the story. How did you solve the problem? Here's what I ended up doing, and here's how I decided what to do. In the case of our teacher, she might say: "First, she is my friend, and friends help friends. Second, I made a promise, and I always to try to keep my promises. So, the first thing I did was call her, and then . . ."

Students need to know how adults solve everyday problems in the real world. If you think you don't have time for this, think again. This exercise is not a waste of time; it is an investment in your students that will pay off later since you're role modeling three things for your class. First, adults have problems and how they deal with them is useful. Second, just because a problem is tough, big, or stressful doesn't mean it is unsolvable. Finally, it is a chance for you to share the process of problem solving. You share your values, your attitude, and the procedures it takes to be a success.

Share Progress on Goals

The last tool for creating a culture of personalization is sharing your personal goals. Many teachers struggle to find a separation between their personal and teacher lives. However, all students, especially those from poverty, love the idea of goals. Setting personal goals and sharing them with your students is an effective way to foster the relational mindset. Post your personal goal in the classroom (since you are asking students to do the same), and share your progress all year (or semester) long. In addition, you'll also post your class goal too.

Sample goals include:

- Participating in community projects
- Starting new eating and exercise habits
- Helping your parents with a goal
- Completing a teaching improvement list
- Running a half-marathon
- Losing weight
- Mentoring someone
- Growing a garden
- Learning a skill or sport (such as martial arts, dance, guitar, or so on)
- Helping change the culture at your school

Share your key milestones and celebrations and how you overcame issues along the way. When you share all the microsteps forward and the nearly predictable setbacks you experience, students will see that mistakes are OK and make way for improvement. Your journey over the course of the year will be a drama akin to must-see TV. In short, as you make progress through obstacles, students can see themselves succeeding and as contributors to your growth. And if you don't have any goals, it's time to start. Your students want a teacher that has kept learning and growing, not a dinosaur who has quit. This is an exciting way to influence students.

Quick Consolidation

This chapter was about a powerful path in your classroom—personalizing teaching. First, learn students' names. Second, create a Me Bag. Third, share everyday problems once a week. Let students learn how to solve them. Then, lastly, share your personal and work goals. As you share part of your life with students, you allow them to understand your journey. Plus, they learn about the process you used, your values, and choices. These three tools are no secret. I'm just inviting you to choose one of these three and make it a habit. Make sure you include each one in your relational toolbox.

CHAPTER 5

CONNECT EVERYONE FOR SUCCESS

In this second of three powerful chapters on the relational mindset, we'll strengthen our skills in connecting everyone, which is at the heart of psychology. Psychologist Daniel Kahneman (as cited in Brockman, 2012) cites connecting with people as one of the few elements that genuinely makes people even happier than money. With that, let's help make your classroom even richer than before.

The Fifty-Fifty Rule

While some teachers work hard to keep students quiet and isolated from their peers, their hard work may be misguided. As students mature from the K–2 years, the genetic drive to connect unfolds. Students want to affiliate with likeminded peers (Lewis & Bates, 2010). Therefore, to effectively impact academic achievement, teachers should split class time equally between social time and individual time—that's the fifty-fifty rule. On any given day, you might split social and individual time seventy-thirty or even ten-ninety, but over a week, it should all even out. Now, a good question is, "Why on earth should I change what I do in my classroom?" Since we all want students to do well academically, let's look at links between social and academic success.

Two key social elements have a strong effect on academic success: (1) belonging and (2) cooperative learning. Research suggests an especially positive and significant relationship between academic achievement and school belonging, and for minority students, a feeling of acceptance (Adelabu, 2007). In fact, a strong feeling of acceptance in class and school helps protect minority students from damaging, environmental social threats (Cook, Purdie-Vaughns, Garcia, & Cohen, 2012). Is your class accepting of others?

One of the more salient differences between the high-achieving students and the underachievers is the presence of supportive peers. Researchers note that even high achievers often experience lulls in their academic success. The high achievers likened the strong peer network to the experience of trying to walk backward down a crowded staircase: "If students started to underachieve and tried to turn and walk down the staircase, many other students pushed them back up the staircase" (Reis, Colbert, & Hébert, 2005, p. 117). Now get ready to get blown away: sixteen of the eighteen high-achieving students told researchers they had strong peer support networks, compared with just *one* of the seventeen *underachievers*.

Second, when cooperative learning is done well, it has an almost magical effect. The effect size of cooperative versus individual learning is 0.59 (Hattie, 2009). This gain is solid; over a year's worth of difference. Additionally, cooperative learning supports the critical feeling of belonging. Most high-performing teachers use one or more of the following social learning strategies: temporary learning partners, long-term study buddies, teamwork, interdependency, or cooperative learning.

Table 5.1 offers strategies for social versus individual time.

Table 5.1: The Fifty-Fifty Rule

Social Time	Individual Time
Cooperative groups and teams	Solo time for journaling and mind mapping
Study buddies or partners to quiz each other	Students practice self-testing
Temporary partners for summarizing time	Goal setting and self-assessment
Learning stations for social data gathering	Reading, reflection, and writing
Group projects for brainstorming and discussion	Seatwork for problem solving

In the next section, we'll take a look at the collaborative activities that enhance social time to connect for success.

Collaborative Activities

Much of what makes social activity work (to the degree it does) is our own biology. We are not just driven to be social. We are genetically timed for it. A baby's entire focus is locking in the best caregiver (mom, dad, grandma, aunt, or so on) around. By age four, children still don't care much about their peers, but they still care a lot about their parents. By mid-elementary school, our genes tell us to start affiliating by making friends. The meanest thing a fourth-grade student can say to another student is, "I'm not going to invite you to my birthday party!" Friends are becoming important, and peers form cliques, clubs, and teams. Students badly want to belong. In school, I remember playing on teams (wrestling, swimming, and basketball) just to be with my friends.

By middle school, we want more than to belong; we want to differentiate. That's the role of status. Secondary students will do (and have done) just about anything to say, "I'm important," "I'm special," "I'm good looking," "I'm smart," or "I'm tough." Why? Social status is hardwired (Zink et al., 2008). The beauty of knowing the biology of your students is that this biology gives openings for building interdependency.

Why does social time work so well? For elementary students, it is fun. Younger students are just learning to have friends, and social learning usually builds connections for social skills as well as academic skills. Students like their friends or peers and enjoy doing things with them. At the secondary level, pride and status are becoming important. Aside from having or making friends, students often don't want to lose face by letting down a friend or classmate. When they need help, there's an affiliated group to offer a hand. In short, the emotional side gets a big boost when you add interdependency to lessons, which makes for more robust effect sizes. *Interdependency* (see figure 5.1) means that student success depends on another student's success, which raises everyone's effort level. Four students in a cooperative group or team has a 0.69 effect size on student achievement (Hattie, 2009). Interdependency can also take the form of study buddies or partners, temporary partners, learning stations, and group projects. To get the goodies out of these social structures, it takes time to build and maintain the relationships.

Figure 5.1: Interdependency builds connections.

Cooperative Groups and Teams

Many teachers will say how groups or teams just waste time. Teams are just structures. By themselves, they will accomplish nothing. Your students need social cues, prompts, and systems to establish and guide behaviors. Let's break down how teams can work. In my middle school classes, teams of five seemed to work best. For elementary school, temporary cooperative groups of four or established teams of four work well. I have drawn the following ideas from many sources (for example, see Kagan, Kagan, & Kagan, 1997).

- **Allow the team to have a unique name, slogan, cheer, celebration, and logo:** This builds social status and camaraderie. Give students time for each of these when building teams.

- **Give everyone a unique and valued role:** Roles engage more of the class and build positive interdependence (examples include summarizer, leader, personal trainer, stretch leader, energizer, joke teller, and courier).

- **Set class norms for all group behaviors:** This reduces students acting out and builds individual accountability. For example, share three things you expect every team to do, such as (1) contribute to the class, (2) be on time, and (3) support each other.

- **Give the group occasional downtime:** This allows for random acts of relationship building and fun. (Limit downtime to two to four minutes.)

- **Ensure the team works together daily:** Use procedures and rituals that involve everyone, every day. Foster equal participation using turn-taking that leadership and group norms regulate.

- **Encourage friendly competition:** This builds teamwork and effort and fosters identity. Consider the following three ways to use friendly competition.

    a.   Student groups or teams can compete against each other when the topic is less academic and more behavioral. For example, what group is the fastest to get cleaned up at the end of class, who has the most team spirit, who will be the first to learn everyone's name in class, who has the best team cheer, or who has the coolest name?

    b.   Students can compete against either the teacher or an outside force (another school, class, or virtual team)—an "us against the world" mentality.

c. Student teams can compete against themselves. They record and display their prior scores or marks, and each week they try to best their last score.

For cooperative groups and teams to be most effective, coach the team leader, and ask him or her to coach and teach the team how to improve. Reciprocal teaching (students teaching peers) has a strong effect size of 0.74 (Hattie, 2009).

Study Buddies or Partners

At the beginning of the year or semester, many teachers set students up with a semi-permanent study buddy who takes responsibility for the success of his or her partner. The students share phone numbers and email addresses so they can call, text, and email. When done well, study buddies tend to form a sibling-like relationship. As a teacher, create stakes in the relationship. Say, "If you want an A or B, you must help your partner get an A or B." If one passes a test and the other does not, it's a shared failure. A teacher who uses this strategy finds it helps students at the secondary level build relationships and learn to help another.

One way to assign study buddies for language arts is to have students write out their passions (such as in the category "What I think needs changing in this world") on an index card. The teacher collects the cards and sorts students into similar interests and passions. That year or semester, students will work with another kindred soul who shares the same passion for change or a specific topic (Henderson, 2012).

If students don't want to work with the partner you assigned, give them some more time and new tools. Allocate relational time in your class to help students get to know their partner. Use simple one- to two-minute activities, and rotate them. For example, students could discuss the following questions.

- What are your academic strengths?
- Where can you use the most help?
- What is the best type of feedback to give you when you are struggling?
- What happened while you were growing up that was important to you?
- How are you best at helping others?

These question activities help students build trust with others and give them a moment to exchange likes and dislikes. Additionally, pairing this activity helps with communication and conflict-resolution skills. Changing partners won't solve the problem if a student doesn't have the social skills to work with a partner.

Here are five basic partner steps for students when practicing conflict resolution.

1. **"I feel"**: "I feel discouraged and disconnected when you don't talk during our partner time."

2. **"When that happens"**: "When that happens, we don't solve problems or learn what we need to know. Yesterday, I really needed help in class."

3. **"I need"**: "I need to know we can work together, can we?"

4. **"Listen"**: Now, the one who just spoke will listen to his or her partner.

5. **"Review and resolve"**: "To review, what you're saying is . . . . To resolve it, how about if we do this one thing differently each time we work together and see what happens?"

Study buddies should sit next to each other in class and share key content as well as be a cheerleader for the other. They will each know the other's progress and be mindful of changes in progress. Both can sign off on this process with their parents and the teacher. Give students time to make plans for what to do next after getting feedback on a quiz or any other formative assessment.

Student mentors are also powerful. Every student needs guidance, encouragement, and leadership. Fourth graders can mentor second graders, eighth graders can mentor sixth graders, and eleventh graders can mentor ninth or tenth graders.

For secondary students, set up a partnership with local colleges or universities for undergraduates to mentor (or tutor) juniors and seniors. For example, undergraduates can tutor students for forty-five minutes after school. Mentoring programs appear to be useful in promoting social relationships (with parents, mentors, or peers) and reducing conflict. High-poverty schools in Los Angeles used collegiate mentors for fourth and fifth graders with solid success (Coller & Kuo, 2014). Other mentoring programs have shown significant positive changes in youths' relationships with parents and teachers and were significantly associated with better youth outcomes, including self-esteem, academic attitudes, prosocial behaviors, and less misconduct (Chan et al., 2013). Check out the appendix (page 185) for several resources about mentoring.

Temporary Partners

Even well-managed teams and partners can get stale, so to freshen up the learning and social experience, teachers can use temporary partners. A simple walk-and-talk activity for elementary or secondary students might go like this: "Oh! I've got a great idea that should only take a minute. Please stand up. Great! Now, when the music begins, and I say, 'Go,' please touch three walls and four chairs that are not your own. Once you get to the spot, wait for further directions. 'Ready, set, go.' Now that you're in a new spot, look around and point to the person nearest you, and say, 'You're it!' If you still need a partner, raise your hand. That new person will be your temporary neighbor for the next sixty seconds. Now that you have a partner, here's your challenge. Earlier we were discussing _____, and it's time to finish that."

You can then introduce the activity, such as students acting out a pro-and-con role, summarizing key points of the lesson, creating deeper and more interesting questions, or sharing what they know and need to learn. Once students finish the activity, they raise their hands. When all students have finished, ask them to thank their partners, using their first names, and head back to their seats. To further engage students, you can use music as a cue to end the activity and move forward.

Quick Consolidation

As we've seen, many forms of interdependency can work to allow students to connect everyone for success. While in earlier chapters, we focused on personalizing the learning, this chapter focused on you getting multiple strategies to link students with one another. The key theme is the fifty-fifty rule, which gives you an approximate time frame for a week's worth of social priorities. Your strategies included cooperative groups and teams, study buddies, and temporary partners. No one method is perfect because, ultimately, students will crave a bit of novelty when they get tired of a social structure. The idea is to develop multiple sources that allow students to work with others in which the stakes are high for the common goals. In your class, part of successful student assessments is how the team (or study buddy) does, so everyone is working together. I have found interdependency to be one of the best tools for classroom success.

CHAPTER 6

SHOW EMPATHY

When I first started teaching secondary students, I was focused more on content than my students. Like many secondary teachers' experiences, my students were who I worked with in order to get results. I wasn't mean (well I did say a few mean things in retrospect), but more important, I just had no clue how important I was, as a person, to my students. Today, one big change you would see and hear with me is that I have developed empathy. The less stability that students have at home, the more they need a caring, trusting adult at school. "Do you care?" is the one of the biggest questions students will ask you. Here's how to answer that question with a reaffirming, "Yes!"

Putting Empathy First

Many teachers struggle with providing students with what they need the most: someone who cares about them and about their school progress. As we know, bad things happen to everyone. However, students from poverty may not have the cognitive skills, emotional support, or coping skills necessary to deal with adversity. The key isn't to be sympathetic but to show empathy and provide tools. You see, sympathy is the ability to understand another with feelings of sorrow for their misfortune. Empathy is a bit different; it is the ability to understand and share the same feelings. I am embarrassed to say this, but I had zero empathy until I was in my thirties and forties. I had to learn it from others. The good news is, empathy can be taught (Schumann, Zaki, & Dweck, 2014).

Quality relationships form the bedrock and foundation of emotional stability. An alarming three out of four students in poverty do not have cohabitating parents at home (U.S. Census Bureau, n.d.a). Students

45

don't need to be told their lives are tough; they often need a caring adult or a shoulder to lean on and an empathic teacher who listens. When students do not get support and empathy, they have more than just hurt feelings; they have stress. Students from poor families typically experience more stressors and have fewer skills to cope with that stress (Evans & Kim, 2007). Minority students are more likely to experience chronic stress (Brody, Lei, Chen, & Miller, 2014).

Some cautious generalizations about the developing brain would be "More brain matter is better than less" and "Clear, high volume pathways are better than inefficient pathways." Nearly everywhere in the brain is critical to our survival, or it would not likely be preserved through our DNA for centuries. Now, why the background on the brain? Surprisingly, the effect of poverty on the brain can be physical as much as mental and emotional. Exposure to poverty during early childhood is associated with smaller white matter, less cortical gray matter (as compared with nonpoor samples), and reduced volume of a key structure (the hippocampus) for learning, memory, and emotional regulation (Hanson, Chandra, Wolfe, & Pollak, 2011). The hippocampus is a crescent-shaped structure located in the lower-central temporal lobe. This structure is highly involved in spatial learning, relevance, and regulating input to long-term memory. When you see students behaving in nonsensical ways in your class, take a deep breath and remember, "When bad things happen, the brain is changed." Just connect and help your students graduate college or career ready.

In addition, simple exposure to parental verbal abuse adversely impacts the brain (Choi, Jeong, Rohan, Polcari, & Teicher, 2009). This exposure to verbal abuse affects the integrity of left hemisphere pathways involved with processing language, as well as fiber tracts involved in emotional regulation. This is now clear biological evidence of a deleterious effect of ridicule and humiliation on brain connectivity.

Now, for some good news; the hippocampus is not fixed or stuck at any size. Positive relational experiences can change it for the better. Our brain structures respond to empathic support by reducing stress hormones (like cortisol) and increasing the serotonin for well-being (Williams, Perrett, Waiter, & Pechey, 2007). When empathy is strong, emotional support fosters greater growth of the hippocampus, which enhances learning and memory. Plus, emotional support builds new mass in this structure, which is healthy (Luby et al., 2012, 2013). See figure 6.1.

If you are struggling to help students learn and behave, this is critical: foster quality, empathic relationships.

Chronic Stress Shrinks Hippocampus; Supportive Relationships Heal It

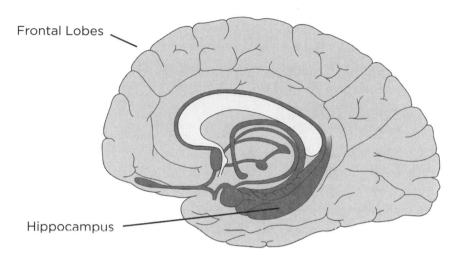

Frontal Lobes

Hippocampus

Source: Hanson et al., 2011; Luby et al., 2012, 2013.

Figure 6.1: Relationships' effect on brain structures.

Using Empathy Tools

When a student shares something adverse that happened, start with empathy first. There are many ways to show you care. Make your caring explicit. Not every student will read your face or body language, which might be your primary way of showing empathy. Here are five empathy-response tools.

1. "I am so sorry to hear that." (Saying this with a sad face shows you care.)
2. "This makes me sick." (Be sad, upset, or very concerned for the student.)
3. "We were worried about you." (Say many others cared about the student; be worried.)
4. "Are you OK?" (Physically check on a student's safety and well-being.)
5. "That's awful. I don't know if I could handle that as well as you are." (This tells the student that the problem was a tough one and that you are showing empathy and admiration.)

I have learned to begin with, "Ohhhh, I am so sorry to hear that." It's curious, even when I am in lousy mood, just saying that triggers empathy. Judging a student's situation gets in the way. Stop telling him or her how to fix it. That comes later, much later. Again, try empathy first.

If a student is in tears because his parents split up or her brother was shot, he or she needs someone to help share the pain, not a lecture about neighborhood risks. Say, "I am so sorry. Let me know what you need, and I'll be there for you." Students who drop out may not be doing well cognitively, but they're far more likely to say, "No one cares."

When it comes to life success, one of the most powerful books is *The 7 Habits of Highly Effective People*. If a student is late for class, remember the first of Stephen R. Covey's (2013) seven habits: seek first to understand. Listen more, and talk less. Before anything else (like a reprimand for tardiness), check for safety. "Are you OK?" Ask what happened without judging. Instead of reprimanding the student, talk privately when you have a chance. Say, "We missed you. Are you OK? Can you talk about what happened?" A lecture about tardiness is unnecessary; make sure students know you *miss them* and *want them* in your awesome class. This is what gets students to show up: when someone cares!

Engage counselors more by telling them about students who need extra support. Counselors can build stronger relationships and help students navigate life and the system. Here's the evidence: when your school adds just one counselor, it increases college attendance by 10 percent (Bouffard, 2014). As you understand the power of connected relationships and the effects of adversity on your students, you'll understand why empathy is critical.

The next time a student doesn't complete an assignment, say, "I'm sorry it didn't get done. Tell me what happened?" The next time a student is late for class, say, "Hey Eric, good to see you. Go ahead and join your teammates. They'll get you caught up." You can talk to him privately a bit later. After a while, ask the student, "Usually you're good about being on time. What happened today?" Remember, seek first to understand, leave the judging aside. To keep coming to school, students need a caring adult, not a judge and an executioner.

Using Quick-Connect Tools

Don't wait until you have friction in your classroom. On day one, students want to know who you are you and whether you care for and respect them. As noted in chapter 4, using student names is a great start to building the class. Many teachers fall short at this. Use the following quick, easy tools to fast-track your relationships with students in your classroom. These are as simple as 1-2-3.

- **One and Done:** In the first thirty days of school, do one favor, make one connection, or show empathy that is so powerful that an individual or whole class remembers it. For example, a student shares a hobby he or she has with you. Let's say it is video games. You go home and search the Internet for the nearest gaming convention dates. Maybe you find a discount coupon online and give it to the student. Because any gift can be misconstrued be sure to ask the student to keep it in confidence.

- **Two for Ten:** Identify one to two students who most need a connection early on. For ten consecutive days, invest two minutes a day in connecting time to talk about anything. This could be right before class, during a seatwork time, or when the student comes up to you for something else. This gives you the relational foundation for the whole semester or year.

- **Three in Thirty:** Ask just enough questions, through any conversation, to discover three things (other than a name) about every student you have in the first thirty days. For example, do you know who else is at home in the family? Do you know what interests the student has outside school? Do you know what the student wants to do when he or she gets older?

Consider the three preceding strategies as a quick start. Additionally, use the following three strategies to show you care: (1) connect early, (2) connect with students' home lives, and (3) connect late.

Connect Early

During the first few minutes, either right before you start or once class has started, make "the rounds" with students. Assess how students are doing on the opening activity, and take a moment to check in with them emotionally. You can build rapport, connect, and show empathy even with brief conversations. Students care more about how much their teacher cares about them than how much the teacher knows.

Some teachers will engage in friendly small talk with students (for example, about their favorite sports team and if that team lost or won). You may politely compliment a student on his or her new hair style or new shoes or ask about an upcoming community event or a family activity. Use the first three to seven minutes to see if anyone is struggling academically and needs extra help.

Connect With Students' Home Lives

There are many ways to widen your relationships with students outside the classroom. Because the time you invest to build relationships with your students is critical, do things early in the year or semester to show you care. On a deeper level, learn about your students' lives (without any judgments) in ways that help foster insights and different ways of thinking, acting, and feeling, as well as an appreciation of where they're coming from. This comes from quality time.

You might attend something that students do after school, such as go to a sporting event, the mall, a movie, a concert, a pick-up basketball game, a funeral, or an activity in the park. Understanding their home lives allows you to show that you really do care. You might be thinking, "This is crazy; I don't have time for that!" But remember, these are investments in the future of your students and the United States. Investing one to two hours early in the year (or semester) can have a big time payback the rest of the year.

Connect Late

When students are leaving class, check their body language. Often their nonverbal signals will indicate their emotional state without you even needing to ask. For example, if a student is dragging himself out of class, maybe he does not want to go to his next class, maybe he does not understand how to do homework, or maybe he is sorting out a big emotional issue. This is the time to check in. Ask, as a student leaves, "Have you got a second?" Then say, "You know I'm always here for you, right? If something's going on, maybe I can help things move along a little easier. What's going on?" Your student will either talk or he or she won't. But at least you reached out. Maybe next time you say that, he or she will open up.

Many high-performing schools, especially secondary, use the last school period for an all-student homework hour. While the research on the value of homework is mixed, at the secondary level, the effect size is strong—0.64 (Hattie, 2009). How can teachers use this time for empathy? Each day, teachers can select a different student to invest a few minutes with—to not just help with homework but to listen and let him or her know you care. If your school does not have this valuable option in place, use classroom seatwork time to connect.

Quick Consolidation

Something shifts when another *gets* you. We feel special, more important, and more connected when another gives us a moment of empathy. That moment says to your students that they are valuable and worth caring for (which might not be the messages they get at home). This chapter gave you a ton of strategies for connecting with students.

When students with troubles at home and personal issues connect with others, they feel more comfortable. Students have to learn they are not alone. Your empathy is price-less. As a teacher you might be the only single human on the planet that will give your students the gift of empathy.

Remember, empathy does not mean you let them off the hook for a bad behavior. It means you care about the student. It means you want to help them get better so that he or she knows better options for next time. It is about you being an ally for how your students feel as much as how they behave. When the teacher is empathetic, you've just added another good reason for your students to come to school, especially to your class.

CHAPTER 7
LOCK IN THE RELATIONAL MINDSET

As I grew up, I knew something was broken but had trouble nailing it down. I don't expect sympathy or blame. I didn't choose my parents, neighborhood, or my upbringing. It took me twenty long years to turn my life around, but I did it. One of many turning points came from reflection: one day, I was reading a book on brain science, introducing the science of human emotional development during our first five years of life. An example in the book (what happens in a person's brain when his or her mother leaves at a young age) was enough to catch my interest, once I saw the consequences in neurobiology. That got me interested in my early life and the brain.

I started to understand why I got in so much trouble at school, why I resisted authority, and why I did not trust my partner in relationships. In time, I was able to sort those things out. I now have empathy for students having a stressful home life, facing daily abuse, or missing a parent. I was one of those kids. I also remember what it was like when things were bad at home, and I know what good teachers meant to me—everything! Teachers who built relationships thought I was a good student. Those who did not build relationships wanted to discard me as a problem and claim they faced their worst nightmare (me acting out) every day. I just needed to see that teachers cared. I would have done anything for them. I wish I could have told them that.

Change the Narrative, Change Your Teaching

Every day you get up and come to work, there's a narrative in your head. The narrative is you making plans for what will happen, what you will do, and how others might respond to you. Now ask yourself, "Was that an average day?"

What if you could have a great day every day? You can, and some people do. But to get there, you'd have to make the changes in your life that would fulfill the criteria for a great day. What would you need to do differently? Would you get up ten minutes earlier? Would you do a brief workout? Eat a smarter breakfast? Learn something new?

The point here is not to tell you what to do. This is all about your daily narratives. Narratives (who you are and what you will do each day) have a high predictability of what will actually happen (Wilson, 2011).

Your narrative is an ongoing story complete with your past, present, and future intentions. When you remember that you have a choice in life, you can change your life story. I changed my story midlife. You can change your students' stories because you are their role model, and you can change your own.

In this part, you saw that students rarely care about passing a test or getting good grades until teachers care about them first. That's right; lock that thought in your brain because relationships really do matter. When you connect, empathize, and care about your students, you will teach well. In each of the upcoming chapters, you'll notice that strong teachers purposefully manage and, when needed, change their narrative. In turn, they also purposefully influence their students' narratives to better their lives. What mindset narrative do you have? See figure 7.1.

You Are Your Mindset: Which Is Yours?

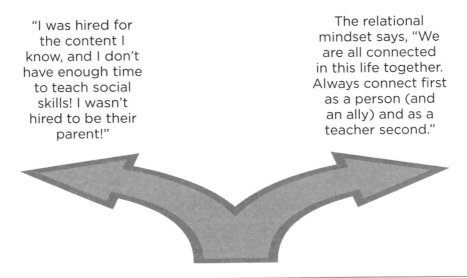

"I was hired for the content I know, and I don't have enough time to teach social skills! I wasn't hired to be their parent!"

The relational mindset says, "We are all connected in this life together. Always connect first as a person (and an ally) and as a teacher second."

Figure 7.1: You are your mindset—the relational mindset.

Fill in the following blanks with your name and a strategy from this mindset. Repeat the phrase daily until it's automatic.

"I, _____, am committing to developing the relational mindset with my students every single day. I will begin with one of the strategies mentioned, which is _____. I will continue this until I have mastery and it's automatic. At that point, I'll learn something new to foster student success."

Reflection and Decision

All meaningful and lasting change starts with a mirror. Self-assess first. Reflect, "Is this topic an issue in my class?" If so, what is the evidence? If not, what is your evidence? Are you ready for a change? In other words, do you want students to graduate job ready or college ready *or not*? In the end, that's what it boils down to, doesn't it?

Your decision to help students grow means that you generate a new narrative that includes the relational mindset. Begin with a fierce urgency, and choose one of the chapters' strategies to get started with better relationships. Encourage colleagues to help, and set goals for progress, using a site such as Stickk (www.stickk.com). Once the message is in your heart, and you've built the activities into your lessons, the mindset will become automatic.

Remember, quality relationships are not a make-or-break situation for every single student and every school. However, for most students from poverty, connections are the only reason they even come to school. Help them make that happen, and enjoy the rewards of the relational mindset.

Quick Consolidation

This part introduced the power of relationships. Many teachers at your school probably assume they were just hired to teach. Yet, research studies conclusively show the value of relationships as a strong academic achievement catalyst. Our relational factors are to, first, personalize the teaching by using names every day and reinforcing them and sharing a piece of yourself at least once a week. Second, connect for success by remembering the fifty-fifty rule. Third, show empathy—respect your students, and don't judge them. Connect with your students outside of school. They need your caring more than you think.

Focus on ensuring that with every contact, every day, your students experience a quality staff relationship. This means every staff member (teachers, counselors, coaches, principals, classroom support, and custodial staff) must know the power of the relational mindset. Remember, put students first, and everything else second.

Will you make mistakes with relationships? Of course. I feel like I made more than my share! It is human to make mistakes. The key is how you deal with the mistake. If you were harsh to a student because you were stressed, make it right with the student. Say, "Hey, can I have a moment? Earlier, I was rude to you, and I am sorry. I was stressed, but that's no excuse; you deserve better. May I consider that I now owe you a favor?"

When you foster trusting relationships rich with support for every student, you'll make a powerful impact on building lives. You can have a classroom and school that has fewer problems and more joy. Plus, your students are more likely to stay in school and graduate. Put relationships first, and you've set the stage for academic success.

PART TWO

WHY THE ACHIEVEMENT MINDSET?

CHAPTER 8

SECRETS OF THE ACHIEVEMENT MINDSET

Most teachers know the potentially dangerous attitude that most students bring to class about mathematics: some just have it, and others don't. Therefore, to get students in the right mindset, Keith Robinson (2013), a savvy mathematics teacher in a high-poverty school, starts class with a video of an Argentine soccer player, the legendary Lionel Messi. It showcases the finest dribbling and game-on-the-line goal-scoring exhibition anyone has ever seen. The students are in awe and await the relevance of Messi to mathematics. Most, even somewhat disinterested students, think Messi is quite talented.

Knowing that he has the students' attention, he then shows a follow-up video. In this video, Messi is doing rigorous, yet quite basic, practice drills. He focuses on fundamentals. He kicks at the goal from every possible angle, often failing over and over again. He misses and then kicks again until he gets it right. More relevant, he's doing this on his own time, during the off-season. Then, the teacher makes the connection: anyone can look cool, but to be awesome, you need practice. You will need to be willing to fail over and over again to become superb.

The teacher's introduction shows students that Messi became one of the best because he was willing to work hard and make a lot of mistakes. That's a key part of school success: show up, work hard, and learn from your mistakes. When students have a fixed mindset and think that some just have it, and others don't, there will be a big problem with achievement. Of course, this same mentality applies to both students and teachers.

The Achievement Mindset

The achievement mindset asks you a simple question: "Are your students' brains stuck for the rest of their life at their current cognitive level or can they be lifted?" If their brains are not stuck, then you are invited (and maybe even compelled) to help each student develop his or her brain better. Obviously, many teachers already do this. They build students' cognitive capacity by teaching vocabulary, writing, reasoning, reading, and organizing skills. They boost motivation by relevant goals, interdependency, and quality feedback. Yes, I am simplifying the process, but you get the idea; these are teachable skills.

The achievement mindset is all about developing student drive, effort, and intention. In this part of the book, you'll learn how to develop steady motivation to help foster student efforts to produce greater achievement by choice. When students are already motivated, it has a solid effect size of 0.48 on achievement (Hattie, 2009). In the following chapters, you'll see how to boost that number. Thousands of U.S. teachers complain that their students lack effort. At the same time, it is a simple fact: a student who appears lazy or unmotivated for one teacher will often work hard for another teacher. This simple fact shows us that the student is different with a different teacher. It is the teaching that makes the difference, and the achievement mindset changes everything. The achievement mindset says, "I can build student effort, motivation, and attitudes to succeed. They are all teachable skills."

> The achievement mindset says, "I can build student effort, motivation, and attitudes to succeed. They are all teachable skills."

Before we try to understand the achievement mindset, let's contrast with some toxic teacher viewpoints, or comments of teachers who struggle with mediocrity.

- "I can push, but most of these students just don't even try."
- "I just don't feel comfortable doing the rah-rah stuff."
- "By this grade, they should be able to motivate themselves. If they can't do it, they're not going to make it anyway."
- "It's not my fault. The parents are supposed to motivate their own students, not me."
- "Motivation is just a gimmick. I focus on the serious stuff. I do content."

These comments will ultimately prevent you from reaching your students. If you blame the students, parents, or your circumstances and make every teaching problem someone else's fault, you're stuck as a professional and won't get better. But if you choose to help your students succeed, you'll bravely hold up a mirror. The mirror reminds all of us, "If it's to be, it's up to me." The achievement mindset shows that when the conditions are right every one of us can and will achieve.

Conversely, with the achievement mindset, a student says, "What I don't know, I can learn. No matter how many obstacles, I can overcome them. If someone else has done this, I can do it too. I will make mistakes and learn from them and persist until I succeed. On top of that, I will not quit!" The achievement mindset shows up in countless high-performing teachers. This mindset leads to teachers making the following comments.

- "In my class, I love teaching students how to motivate themselves. They get so psyched about it, and I love to see them grow."
- "I know just how hard to push and when to give a hand up. My students love the challenge."
- "Sometimes my class feels a bit like a pep rally, but my students need it."
- "The best part is near the end of class when students look at each other and say, 'Wow, we did it!'"

In addition, the questions you ask yourself help make the difference between having low- or high-performing students. Each question invites a specific path of beliefs or actions. These, in turn, begin the process of helping or hurting students' chances for success. The powerful questions become: "When students from higher-risk backgrounds achieve, what did I do to make that happen? When students from higher-risk backgrounds fail, how can I respond differently to help them succeed next time?"

When students succeed, you'll want to consistently attribute it to their preparation, effort, planning, strategies, focus, positive attitude, and persistence—elements under a student's control. Therefore, when students fail, avoid saying the following statements.

- "Well, that's a shame. Maybe you're just not cut out to do this."
- "Bless your heart. You tried so hard."
- "Don't worry about it; I was bad at mathematics too."
- "That's too bad. At least you have other strengths."

Those expressions are known as comfort words for failure, and they are detrimental. In fact, when you say those phrases, it lowers the student's expectations of himself or herself, motivation drops, and the student actually does worse (Rattan, Good, & Dweck, 2012).

The achievement mindset is a way to combat these detrimental statements. It's a combination of Carol Dweck's (2008) growth mindset, Daniel Pink's (2009) drive mindset, Angela Duckworth's (Robertson-Kraft & Duckworth, 2014) and Paul Tough's (2012) grit mindset, and my own work. Yes, I do stand humbly on the shoulders of giants. Each of these mindsets is powerful, but when combined with each other and with highly effective classroom strategies, your success is almost ensured.

A Hard Look at the Evidence

What is the number-one reason for you to buy into the potential to teach the achievement mindset? It is the real-world evidence that strong teachers exhibit each and every day. I can name teacher after teacher with the achievement mindset, and I'll bet you can too. The second best reason is that your students' brains are designed to respond to environmental stimuli (Draganski et al., 2004; Lee et al., 2014; May et al., 2007; Stewart et al., 2003). When you introduce new stimuli, the brain responds. So, when you introduce a different mindset in the right way, students can learn it (Job, Walton, Bernecker, & Dweck, 2015).

So how are these changes being made in the brain? Let's find out what you already know. Following are three common motivator tools in the classroom (Hattie & Timperley, 2007). Please rank each of these on their strength (low, medium, or high) as it contributes to student achievement.

1. **Using rewards:** "Do _____ to get _____."
2. **Using adverse consequences:** "If you do that, bad things will happen. For example, . . .")
3. **Praising student work:** "Good job!"

Each of these statements has an effect size between 0.11 and 0.30 (that's pretty low). It's time to stop doing what is not working. In short, rewards, threats, and bland praise don't get the job done. As a teacher, I plead guilty to having used all of those. How about you?

The teacher's mindset is a critical approach in the art of getting students to succeed (Elliot & Dweck, 2005). In fact, even more than IQ, socioeconomic status, or reading ability, the teacher's mindset predicts student success (Tough, 2012). The mindsets of struggling teachers commonly create a stifling stranglehold on student achievement. Many teachers unconsciously use outdated methods, such as behaviorism, social class, race, or IQ, as a biasing limiter on their own expectations, which then influences their students (Amodio et al., 2004; Rosenthal & Jacobson, 1992). But *you* can be different. Items one through three in the preceding list were weak. Here's how to change the student responses.

Learn the Invisible Motivators

A more contemporary approach to education reveals that to motivate students, you'll want to start paying attention to and digging into how you shape students' achievement mindsets. Why? Build the mindsets, and you'll get better achievement (Cimpian, Arce, Markman, & Dweck, 2007; Grant & Dweck, 2003; R. R. Jackson, 2011).

The fact is that our brain is designed to pick up countless social, physical, and linguistic cues. In some cases, it is the aggregate of factors that you use that makes the miracle happen. Every one of these factors can be a tipping point for student energy, motivation, and effort. While I won't go deeply into each of the following seventeen factors, they do matter a great deal. You can become an amazing motivator when you learn how to use just a few of these brain-smart motivators.

1. **Approach, frame, and define the task appropriately:** Call a task an *experiment* and you may get better results than if you call it a *test*.

2. **Manage the self-talk from you and the student:** Teach students what to say to themselves when they are stuck and struggling such as, "Some things are hard; I can do this."

3. **Show how others have succeeded in the task:** Invite either past graduates or people with the same demographics with a good success story to class.

4. **Make the task worth doing (or not) with high relevancy:** Connect the task to something students care about—"Hey that same kind of effort is what it's going to take when you go looking for that job you said you wanted."

5. **Offer the right type of praise and affirmation:** Forget saying "Good job!" and instead tell the student where he or she is at ("You got 12 of 16 right"), reinforce the mission ("You are at 75 percent, closing in on 100 percent"), and ask for the student's plan to get to the goal.

6. **Orchestrate the autonomy and ideal social conditions:** Give choices, and set up interdependency with either a team or study partner.

7. **Teach students how to deal with obstacles and criticism:** Let them prepare a response for when others criticize, then have them practice it while being dissed.

8. **Purposely develop grit to keep trying a task:** Define grit, point it out when it occurs, give examples of it, talk about you using it in your own life, and give long-term projects.

9. **Inspire a sense of mastery to do well:** Show awe and admiration for excellence, and then help students see models of quality work.

10. **Provide core background subskills needed for the task:** Identify one to two skills that would make the whole task much easier and embed them in the daily work (such as subject-specific study skills, working memory skills, or study skills).

11. **Orchestrate positive emotions into the task and celebrate:** Stop the class, and do a brief three- to five-second celebration for micro milestones or class successes; use music and team leaders to model the celebrations.

12. **Identify stereotype threats and remove them:** Especially for women and minorities, help them reframe negative feedback as well as teach the whole group about the issues.

13. **Provide the most effective types of quality feedback:** Emphasize a student's strategy, effort, or attitude for qualitative and quantitative feedback; ask "Where are you at?" with "What's your goal?" and "How will you get there?"

14. **Frame failures so students grow from them:** Role-model how to handle failures, and give students a template for doing this in the classroom.

15. **Build relationships so students will listen to you:** As noted, building relationships with students is important. Revisit strategies that have been discussed so far.

16. **Help students set much higher goals with microsteps:** Set only two kinds of goals—the huge gutsy goals for the long haul and the next-week goals (micro goals). (See chapter 9, page 69.)

17. **Build subject-specific study skills:** If you teach mathematics, use a step-by-step process that is a generic guide for all mathematics problems posted in your class.

Honestly, not all of the preceding items are on every teacher's radar, and that's no surprise. I didn't think about those factors years ago either. In the next few chapters, you'll learn to embrace several of these elements to begin the shift in classroom motivation.

Foster a Growth Mindset

Let's start with a typically uninspired and tough student group—adolescent mathematics students. Lisa Blackwell, Kali Trzesniewski, and Carol Dweck's (2007) two-year longitudinal study examined two groups of students. One group was given a growth mindset (students were told intelligence is malleable, not fixed) and another group was given a fixed mindset (students were told research confirms intelligence is stable). Students with a growth mindset outperformed the other group on test scores and had more effort and interest over three times as often. Figure 8.1 shows differences between these two groups: having a growth mindset influences scores by 4 percent two years after intervention. Yes, mindsets are teachable.

Another study shows that early skill development in disadvantaged students leads to more motivation and a large percentage of students succeeding later in life, in regard to school achievement, employment, advanced degrees, and homeownership (Knudsen, Heckman, Cameron, & Shonkoff, 2006).

Growth Mindset Versus Fixed Mindset

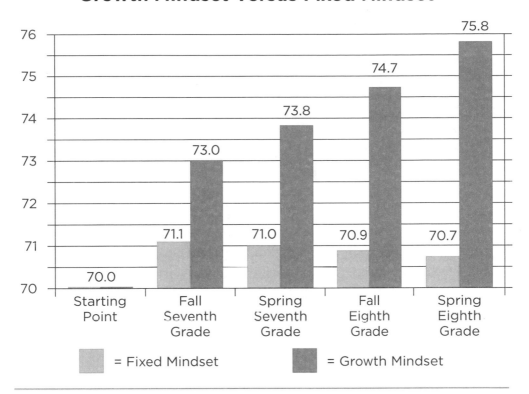

Figure 8.1: Middle school mathematics mindset influences scores.

Alternatively, what hurts performance is the effect of stereotype threat—when students feel stereotyped due to religious, ethnic, or gender bias. This bias can cripple a student's academic achievement scores unless dealt with. Ultimately, it is the unresolved emotions (fear, anger, disgust, sadness, or so on) within a student that hinders the cognitive capacity, resulting in lower scores (Mangels, Good, Whiteman, Maniscalco, & Dweck, 2012). Emotion blocks the path to learning under stereotype threat. The good news is that you can prevent stereotype threat by how you address the issues upfront. For example, telling students that their feelings are justified and giving them coping tools will decrease the effects.

Do you think IQ is fixed? Small motivators even influence IQ scores. In a meta-analysis of random-assignment experiments, material incentives (money, tokens, and candy) increased IQ scores by an average of 0.64 standard deviations. This suggests that our attitudes and drive can influence scores quite a bit under low-stakes conditions. Incentives actually increased IQ scores by 0.96 (almost a full standard deviation) among students with below-average IQs over baseline (Duckworth, Quinn, Lynam, Loeber, & Stouthamer-Loeber, 2011).

Drop the Labels

Motivation is rarely in the *pep talk* category. It is actually a carefully targeted message, spoken with love, that pulls out of each student his or her deepest drive to move forward. It means that the little things do matter. I am grateful for the guidance from Yvette Jackson (2011) on this matter. For example, drop the following labels from your vocabulary.

- *Minority students*: Latino, African American, and Asian students make up 50.3 percent of U.S. public K–12 classrooms (Maxwell, 2014). Therefore, they are the majority school population. Calling these students *minorities* implies they have less power. Use the name for the ethnicity you are referring to, such as *African American*.

- *Low achievers* or simply *low students*: These terms imply some sort of deficit when the real truth is that the student may have had underperforming teachers for several years. A student may "underperform" as compared to the district mean, if that's your reference point.

- *Disadvantaged* or *disabled students*: Students from poverty are more likely to be school dependent for their enrichment, and many are inappropriately labeled as disabled when in fact, they have poverty-related differences, such as stress disorders, or unaware teachers.

Quick Consolidation

In this chapter, you explored research on human motivation and drive that turns one hundred years of behaviorism upside down. Teachers can no longer promote classroom gimmicks or use rewards and punishments and expect them to build long-term motivation or grit. You've discovered some important points.

First, the student's mindset matters. When students are not behaving in a motivating way, avoid blaming the student. Second, the mindset is teachable. Change what you're doing, and start influencing the student's achievement mindset. Naturally, you'll want to reflect on you own. Any time you think a student has a fixed mindset, remind him or her that brains can change when he or she simply changes the strategy, effort, or attitude. Now, it's time to dig into four of the most effective achievement boosters of all time.

1. Set gutsy goals.
2. Have the right attitude.
3. Give fabulous feedback.
4. Persist with grit.

The upcoming chapters will introduce these four achievement boosters. There is no ascending or descending order of importance. In fact, these ideas play off each other with a synergistic effect. Your favorite idea may even be in another chapter. After all, an achievement-boosting strategy may also contribute to class climate or energy.

Be patient in building the class campfire of energy. Every spark you bring to the classroom campfire will build the student fires of desire. The content you teach might remain the same. However, the circumstances for learning, your context, and your strategies can create highly motivated students, if you know how to do it. Get psyched; coming up are specific and practical ways you can build student effort, student achievement, and a passion for learning.

CHAPTER 9

SET GUTSY GOALS

What would you predict is the greatest single contributing factor to student achievement? Would you say parental support, genes, or school quality? Would you guess effort, past achievement, or socioeconomic status? Any of those would be a pretty good guess. But there's a factor that is worth more than those. In fact, this factor contributes almost three years' worth of gains. The problem is most teachers don't know what it is. Worse, when many teachers hear the answer, they'll dismiss it. Will you?

The research is solid. Students' self-reported grades and expectations of their success (or failure) in class have a whopping effect size of 1.44, ranking it near the top of all contributors to student achievement (Hattie, 2009), contributing to nearly three years of growth. Low-performing students expect (based on their own past performance) to struggle or fail at school each year. That's why high-performing teachers never allow students' low expectations to become the norm. Starting the first day of school, strong teachers encourage students to set the long-term bar sky-high. Students having some control over more short-term goals has an effect size of 1.21 (Willett, Yamashita, & Anderson, 1983). Later, I'll show you why students also need a reason to buy into it.

For example, if you ask a student who has failed in mathematics for three years in a row his or her goal, it would likely be to just pass. But that student goal will not cut it in a high-performing teacher's class where goals are advanced or expert level, not just basic proficiency. This is why asking students to set their own long-term goals can be dicey among those who have previously struggled. Effective teachers create the climate and the expectations starting on day one and never, ever back off them.

You might say, "But what if the student does not work hard?" Actually, whether a student works hard, or not, is a choice the student makes, and it is not genetic. It is based on a host of factors, but these four factors are near the top of the list (Dweck, 2002; Stipek, 2002).

1. Students' prediction of whether success is possible and expectancy of personal success based on their past
2. Their perceptions about their teacher's capacity to help them succeed
3. Students' self-assessment
4. Their overall self-concept

The good news is you can influence every single one of these four factors. That's why teachers who struggle say, "Students don't even try." However, teachers who succeed regularly shift student perceptions about what is possible, show students that their own teacher is highly capable, tell students that their past is not their future, help build a new narrative to strengthen their self-concept as a success, and finally, provide students with the tools and climate to succeed. Let's begin with tools for greater expectations.

Creating Gutsy Goals for Mastery

Gutsy goals are jaw-dropping, nearly impossible, shoot-for-the-stars milestones. In 1962, President Kennedy's gutsy national goal was to land a man on the moon and return him safely before the end of the decade (Kennedy, 1962), which the United States achieved in 1969. However, he set the goal before the science had even been invented to reach the goal.

Gutsy goals are a concrete and exciting way to focus on mastery. Get students pumped up about something far greater than finishing a chapter in a textbook. Why would you set goals you might not reach? James Cameron, director of two of the highest-grossing films of all time (*Titanic* and *Avatar*), said we should set impossibly high goals so that when we fail, we will fail above others' successes (as cited in Goodyear, 2009). For teachers, this means setting goals of mastery, not merely basic understanding or proficiency.

If you are serious about developing ambition and achievement in your students, teach them how to set higher, gutsier goals. After all, either you believe the brain can change or not. Either you believe you're good at your job or not. Remember, even modest, achievable goals have a positive 0.52 effect size (one year's gain). But it's better to go higher. Stop being afraid to fail, and start being bold enough to sell your students on their real potential. High-performing, high-poverty schools have this core achievement driver (mastery, not basic or proficiency levels) in common, and it's a must for your classroom (Johnson, Uline, & Perez, 2014). The bottom line is this: great teachers typically set big goals for their students (Farr, 2010).

The mastery process is one where a teacher says, "I don't just want them to get it right. I want them to become so proficient that they can't get it wrong. Only then will we move on." The mastery process is not just about content. It's about helping students develop lifelong competencies, such as grit and perseverance, social skills, cognitive skills, and classroom behaviors that make complex, challenging learning worthwhile.

You might say, "This goal-setting factor is just good teaching. We all know that." But in mastery, there is no personal best or just good enough. Mastery typically includes setting very high challenging goals that the student may or may not be capable of reaching at all. Mastery as a goal has a huge 0.96 effect size (two years of growth) for disadvantaged and lower-ability students (Kulik & Kulik, 1987).

Mastery can take an extra 10 to 50 percent more classroom time (which is always at a premium). This classroom time is typically invested on more varied uses of a new skill, under differing conditions, first solo, then with partners, as well as invoking more stressful conditions. However, the extra time can pay off dramatically in improved student performance over time. Plus there's less wasted time spent with ongoing reteaching.

The goal is the process, as well as the destination. These are goals that cannot be met, until you grow into one who can reach them. Gutsy goals are revised SMART goals (Conzemius & O'Neill, 2014).

- Specific and strategic
- Measurable
- Amazing (rather than *attainable*)
- Relevant
- Time bound

Setting Gutsy Goals

Growing up in the digital generation, most students feel like anything they need in the world can be gained through short, nearly instant grabs. For example, when they need a fact or answer, students often google it. All of this shallow learning is nearly instantaneous, and the gratification is split-second fast. However, becoming a good learner requires the capacity to dig deeply into a topic, which requires having persistence, thinking about it, clarifying it, analyzing it, and developing a complex, yet clear, understanding. This is hard work, and most students don't know how to do it. Yet, in higher-performing urban schools, the deeper, mastery learning is a key part of the solution (Johnson et al., 2014). In order to truly have a consistent achievement mindset, you must have something special worth doing. In that classroom, student goals should produce something of value—something that is personally or culturally relevant—and be part of something bigger than themselves.

Teachers become more positive when students show sustained effort when seeking nearly impossible goals and find purpose and meaning (Fredrickson et al., 2013). There are several salient features about setting gutsy goals. First, when you create gutsy goals for your students, you must get inside their head. You must know what they care about and how much it matters. The goal must have specificity for a big impact (0.94 effect size; Marzano, 1998). Second, you must tell them why they can believe in you and the goals you have set. Finally, you'll need to set micro goals (see page 75) so they can get concrete evidence that the gutsy goals are happening.

You're not saying it's easy. However, setting low goals (like "Be ready for class each day") that your students can reach with little or no effort diminishes a student's potential to achieve. It sells everyone short including you. Go for the stars. Let's learn how to create high class expectations with high goals to get students to the promised land of consistent high effort. Following are elementary and secondary examples of gutsy goals.

Elementary Teacher Examples

Let's say that last year a teacher had 50 percent of her students reach proficiency in mathematics. I have heard those teachers set what seems like lofty new goals for class like, "At least 80 percent of my students will be proficient in mathematics, and 20 percent or more will get to mastery level." These might be higher goals than you've ever had before, but sorry, they are not gutsy goals. Here's a gutsy goal: "My first-grade students will read, write, do mathematics, and behave so that by the end of the year, they are ready for third grade, not second." This goal makes two years of gains with your students.

I have also heard teacher goals like, "This year, all my students will reach their potential." Unless you have a specific way to measure your students' potential, how would you know what their potential is? A nine-year-old (Dylan Mahalingam) has spoken before the United Nations (Edcoogle, 2014). A seventeen-year-old (Malala Yousafzai) was awarded the Nobel Peace Prize (Edcoogle, 2014). Wouldn't that be more in tune with your students' potential? That's why a gutsy goal is important; it is for the student who just might reach it.

Remember, if you work in a school with high-poverty students, getting one and a half to three years of academic progress per year is basic progress. Without very aggressive goals, you increase the likelihood for students to drop out or fail. Make your own goals jaw-dropping, amazing, and unlikely (but possible) to reach. Here are examples of teacher gutsy goals.

- **A process goal:** "This year, I will engage my students every nine minutes or less for the entire year."
- **A relational goal:** "This year, I will learn at least three things (outside of a name) about every student, and I'll do a One and Done (from chapter 6) with my two class leaders in the first thirty days."

- **A result goal:** "My second-grade students will read, write, do mathematics, and behave so that by the end of the year, they are ready for fourth grade, not third."

Secondary Teacher Examples

Let your students know about your own gutsy goals. You'll want to set goals so high that you're unlikely to (but maybe you might) reach them. That sends a message to your students to shoot for the stars.

- **A process goal:** One science teacher's goal might be, "I will teach my students how to rebuild a city from scratch when disaster strikes." One middle school English teacher might ask her students to write a paper to change the world. Their final papers could be read to community leaders, and the feedback would be life changing.
- **A relational goal:** "I will complete a One and Done with one or two students in every class and do name-learning activities until every student knows every other student by first name."
- **A result goal:** "I will get two years of academic progress for every year I teach" or "I will become a top 50 finalist for the Fishman Prize for Superlative Classroom Practice."

Student Examples

Here are student examples for gutsy goals. It's important for students to share their goals with you and each other as well.

- **A process goal:** "I will read at least five pages a day and take at least two pages of notes every school day of the year."
- **A relational goal:** "I will know every other student in class by first name."
- **A result goal:** "I will get an A or B in every class."

Giving a Reason to Believe

When you share gutsy goals, those around may be tempted to roll their eyes. It is as if they are saying, "Yeah, sure, right; like that's going to happen." That's why you'll give students a reason to believe in you. Big goals *sound good*, but unless you can back them up, you will lose your followers. How you do this is critical. Let's visit those who already do this well—high-performing teachers.

Jamie Irish, a high school mathematics teacher in New Orleans, sets two gutsy goals. One goal is to beat the scores of a nearby, more affluent school, Lusher Charter School (Irish, 2012). He also sets a gutsy goal of being able to beat a particular mathematics score on a college entrance test. To *sell* students on why the first goal is important, he says Lusher is a selective-admission school that consistently ranks in the top ten in the state because almost all students score either mastery or advanced on the Louisiana Educational Assessment Program (the state's high-stakes test administered in fourth and eighth grades). He also says that most Lusher students go on to attend top colleges, which is why a basic competency is not good enough. He leads his class on a mission to *crush* Lusher from day one. His teaching goal on day one is to expose the fallacy that passing is acceptable. The new student goal is advanced proficiency. He creates a tangible opposition (Lusher) and tangible reward (free tuition to college) when test scores are high. To affirm it, his whole class reads a newspaper article together that documents the correlations of LEAP scores with later ACT college entrance scores. For students to qualify for a scholarship providing free tuition to in-state universities, they know they must score at advanced on the ACT. He is creating greater expectations and giving them a reason to buy into them. Now the students know why basic is too low.

All semester long, he says, in essence, to his students, "This goal we have is critically important. I know you can do it with smart effort. I care about you. I care about your education. I will not give up on you. I will reteach this as many times as needed until everyone gets it. Because we are all in this together, if one of us fails, we all fail—and that includes me." Through these statements, the teacher shows students the goal is worth their time, and he affirms their capacity to succeed, their relationship, and resolve.

Gutsy goals take work. You must give students a reason to believe it's possible and then show how it can happen. If you don't do this second step, two things happen. First, you may stop believing in yourself. Second, your students may not believe you either. A reason to believe is critical.

Check out the following twenty-second "Why you should believe in me" segments to help students believe in you.

- "Here's why we have such high goals. First, I care about you and want you to succeed. Second, I will work harder, use better ideas, and grow to become your best teacher ever. When you and I work as a team, we all can succeed."

- "I care about you, I'm good at what I do, and I'll work hard, persist, and learn from my mistakes. You do your part, and I guarantee I'll do my part. I won't let any of you fail. Now, let's get to work!"

- "Do you know why you'll reach your goals? Because I won't let you fail. You do your part, and I promise I'll do my part. I'm good at what I do and will work to ensure you succeed. Together, we are unstoppable."

Did you ever have a teacher say these to you in school? I didn't. That kind of confidence can move mountains. Gutsy goals are specific, relevant, and crazy high. Gutsy goals should be nearly impossible, and they should ask you to grow into a different person in order to reach them. It is better to set outrageously high goals and fall short, than set low ones, succeed, and pretend that you've just been named the MVP of the Super Bowl.

Reinforce the gutsy goals weekly, so that students can visualize them, hear them echo in their minds, and feel them viscerally. Post reminders and encourage students to talk to others about them. Many teachers (at both elementary and secondary levels) post college banners around the classroom. These are inspiring, especially if you write the names of past students who have gone on to that college below the banners. That's inspiration; can you do that? Unless you help students understand that it is the pursuit of the goals that makes life worthwhile—and that we all will encounter temporary failures—they may quit on you and on themselves.

Finally, and maybe most importantly, help teach students how to deal with failure. Tell them that failure is part of life and part of progress. Remind them often that failure is simply feedback on what did not work. Failures are lessons. Failures teach us. They can be positive when we positively accept and learn from them. How we respond to failure defines us, not the encounter itself. Getting knocked down is nothing; getting back up is everything. Students will get back up if their vision of worthwhile goals is strong enough and they have reinforcement along the way. That's where micro goals come in.

Using Micro Goals to Close the Gaps

For most students, having gutsy goals is exciting. However, it's difficult to reactivate the long-term sky-high goals over and over on cue. Any of us would find it hard to stay psyched about a goal that seems so far away. Training for the Olympics or trying to get an advanced degree are big motivators, but still, we all need those hourly, daily, and weekly nudges to keep us going. It is the trail of emotional highs that keep us moving forward, not the once-a-year goal.

That's why you'll need to constantly set micro goals that your students can reach within a week or less. These specific, concrete goals can:

1. Reaffirm a specific competency
2. Give measurable progress toward the gutsy goals
3. Provide a quick emotional affirmation and moment for a celebration

Because micro goals allow students to get immediate feedback for themselves, the effect size is a sizzling 0.97 (Marzano, Pickering, & Pollock, 2001). That's almost two years' worth of gains! Set daily and weekly goals that students can reach with a solid effort. This step is critical. They need to see that they can reach the big gutsy goals, one bite at a time. When students set their own micro goals, the effect size is a strong 1.21—well over two years' worth of academic progress (Marzano et al., 2001). Although adults understand the power of greater expectations, students will use their past experiences to set goals and often set them too low. However, they don't know how far they can go with an amazing teacher (like you). You can help them set and link the micro goal completion to the bigger gutsy goal. Then, every week, check in on your goal progress. See figure 9.1.

Gutsy goal: *Finish fifth grade ready for seventh grade.*	
Week One	Micro Goal
✓	*Get 100 percent proficiency this week.*
Week Two	Micro Goal
	Be 100 percent on time every day.

Figure 9.1: Micro goal checklist.

Visit **go.solution-tree.com/instruction** *for a free reproducible version of this figure.*

Remember that some weeks are dedicated to holidays, tests, or professional development, so you'll have to include these additions in your achievement calendar.

Many students will get discouraged on this path because they will hit obstacles. For some, they may interpret the roadblocks as a lack of ability. This is why you must continually build the growth mindset ("Your brain can change. IQ can change. Take three continuous steps forward. The one-step setbacks are temporary, and they're simply feedback to help you discover a better way"). Unless you're proactive in this, the setbacks will change everything.

Students often respond differently to learning versus performance goals. Students focused on mastery-oriented learning are also focused on learning and growing. However, that path inspires an entirely different thought process than performance goals, which can be risky unless students have the growth mindset (Smiley & Dweck, 1994; Dweck, 2008). As long as public policy is focused on performance goals for students, teaching the achievement mindset is a must. Your own goals are to keep students pushing themselves forward.

Lastly, assume the best of your students. Always pursue the gutsy goals with a high expectation for mastery. When students get questions right or reach their micro goal, celebrate and continue interacting for even higher-order learning. There is always room for improvement. If they struggle, help them uncover the false assumptions or strategies. Help them grow. Most students learn how to play the classroom game of being safe: "Just say what the teacher wants to hear." Do not let them sink to that level. Higher learning requires not only the achievement mindset but also the emotional safety for a relentless intellectual curiosity. If you give up on students, they'll quit too.

Quick Consolidation

This chapter has been about gutsy goals. The starting point is to set them crazy high, quantify them, and keep them simple. Then, give us a reason to believe in you. Finally, set your micro goals so that you can get feedback on the way to reaching your gutsy goals.

There are two primary reasons that most teachers do not set gutsy goals. One, they do not know how valuable gutsy goals are in inspiring student achievement. Second, they are afraid that if they set goals too high, students won't reach them and they'll feel like failures. Life is too short to fear failure. Every one of the most amazing successes in history had many failures. Do you think of Michael Jordan as a success or failure? Michael Jordan missed twenty-six game-winning shots (JayMJ23, 2006). What we remember were his successes. Every time your class reaches a micro goal, pause for quick celebrations, saying, "Hey class, we did it! We are one step closer to our big goal this year." Celebrations are important because they promote the values and standards that are fundamental to your class.

Before you go any further, write out your gutsy goals for you and your students. Be specific.

_____

_____

_____

_____

_____

_____

CHAPTER 10

HAVE THE RIGHT ATTITUDE

As you've discovered, building student achievement can be a challenge. So far, you've set gutsy and micro goals. Now, we continue the process with the more hidden side of achievement: the attitudes. Commonly, teachers think of attitudes as if they are permanent, but they're not. There was a period in my own life (late twenties) when I was probably the most negative and cynical I have ever been. My daily language was peppered with profanity, and my outlook was cynical. What changed? I met great role models who showed me another way. These two role models became my mentors, and I am forever grateful for them. Without them, I just don't know how things would have worked out. Once my attitude changed, everything else changed for the better.

This chapter will introduce you to a new way of thinking about student achievement. Here are four primary tools: (1) modeling the achievement mindset, (2) modeling high-achievement thinking, (3) sowing the seeds of success, and (4) attributing connections. Each of these tools goes after our thinking and behaviors in a different way. Each can be life changing, so let's get started.

Model the Achievement Mindset

Two scientific discoveries reinforce the power of modeling the achievement mindset: (1) the discovery of mirror neurons and (2) the transmission of affect. The first is generally more neurobehavioral, and the second is usually more social and emotional. Together, these make a case for why upbeat, positive teachers will more likely have positive students and why grumpy teachers with personal problems are less likely to inspire their students.

Discovery of Mirror Neurons

It was a typical summer day in the mid-1990s at Parma University, Italy. Inside a research facility, macaque monkeys sat bored in a lab while the scientists took a lunch break. The monkeys had been wired up to register brain cell firings for planning and registering movement. When a student researcher returned from lunch, he was holding an ice cream cone and lifting it to his mouth to eat. Suddenly, the monkeys' brain cells lit up and buzzed like crazy. At first, no one understood what was happening. Then, over time, the scientists realized that the monkeys were mimicking and rehearsing the human movements. This was the beginning of the discovery of imitation or what we know as mirror neurons.

The monkeys learned what to do based on watching the researchers. More interesting, specific neurons activated each time they imitated researchers. Later, researchers found that mirror neurons are visually receptive to automatic imitation and empathy (Lamm, Batson, & Decety, 2007; Molenberghs, Cunnington, & Mattingley, 2009). Furthermore, these neurons are an associative way humans (and other animals) learn from others. These imitation responses function most strongly when we are either in a goal-directed state ("I want to do what she is doing") or when we are oblivious to our surroundings and the imitation is peripheral (like contagious yawning in a group). In short, some of what your students do in class may be the "monkey see, monkey do" phenomenon. This, in nutshell, is why your role modeling matters.

Transmission of Affect

The *transmission of affect* (Brennan, 2004) describes the transfer process through emotions. This process is social in origin but biological and physical in effect. When we are around others, we may feel either warm or cold toward them. We may feel empathic based on an immediate (often unconscious) judgment. In a stressful situation, we may be able to cut the tension with a knife, so to speak. This understanding means we are not self-contained in our effects, and we are part of and, simultaneously, cocreating the environment.

Everything you say, do, or attend to can influence another's stress level, pheromones, or emotions. These biological changes catalyze peoples' judgments and memories (Kohl, 2012; Miller & Maner, 2010; Steiger, Haberer, & Müller, 2011). Your students will feel good about learning and school based partly on how the carrier (you) is transmitting affect. "I like that teacher," a student says.

Part of the reason for this type of processing of others is that our brains are designed for a social-emotional experience. That's part of our survival. That includes reading others, making decisions about whether to socialize and to what degree, and evoking feelings about each situation. As one enters the company of others, there's an instant sociological and neurological effect. We process the presence of facial expressions, auditory signals, visual messages, pheromones, threats, and affiliations, which in turn, affect ourselves. However, our brain's most basic, yet dominant, communications are the distribution of our hormones and peptides, not the cognitive information. In short, these nonverbal communications are happening on a broad, unspoken chemical level, which produce the gut reactions and the subtle feeling that something is true or false. That's part of the transmission of affect.

When others pick up on your positive emotions, good things happen. Experiments have shown that induced positive affect widens the scope of attention (Rowe, Hirsh, & Anderson, 2007), broadens behavioral repertoires (Fredrickson & Branigan, 2005), and increases intuition (Bolte, Goschke, & Kuhl, 2003) and creativity (Isen, Daubman, & Nowicki, 1987). Now, let's find out how you can boost the achievement mindset too.

Model High-Achievement Thinking

Most teachers feel a bit like actors—we perform on stage (or in the classroom) in front of a live audience. I thought I could live with that truism until I started watching videos and seeing pictures of how I presented myself throughout the day. Truth is, I found it humbling and discouraging. Ultimately, using my growth mindset, I said, "You've got to improve your communications, gestures, and language; they're terrible!" Now, I am far from a celebrity, but I have become much more purposeful. Here are a few strategies that have helped me model high-achievement thinking.

- **Start with a smile and positive greeting:** An amazing number of teachers start with an assignment, directions, a complaint, a demand, or a correction. That's a terrible way to build achievement. Make it a personal mandate to start every day off well.

- **Show you are happy with student progress:** Even if you feel a bit over the top, go ahead and jump, clap, put a smile on your face, and let students know that you *live* for their success.

- **Smile more than you think you need to:** I remember a student who stayed after class and said "I don't understand why you don't like me." At first I was flabbergasted. I had hardly interacted with her. I certainly did not dislike her. Then, she explained how she knew I disliked her. She revealed a subtle list of cues, a look, misdirected attention, and body language. When she finished, I was saddened and humbled. I knew I had so much more work to do as a teacher. From her perspective, she was right; and that perspective was the only one that mattered.

To model high-achievement thinking, Jamie, our New Orleans teacher introduced in chapter 9, rewards his students who succeed in "crushing Lusher." He rewards, recognizes, and celebrates all students' success. Using a Heisman Hopefuls bulletin board, he posts students' assessments under three subheadings: (1) All-American, (2) All-State, and (3) All-City. Students strive to score 100 percent to get their names posted underneath All-American.

Sow the Seeds of Success

We know what exposure looks like. We hear songs on the radio and decide to download them. We see products in movies and find ourselves buying them a month later. We are all so used to this marketing since it's part of our everyday lives. So the point for the classroom is simple: how much exposure do you give students to sell a compelling future? Here are some ideas to follow up on at your school.

- Use phrases such as, "When you graduate . . ."
- Post pictures of graduates at work or in college to make success real.
- Offer T-shirts that say "Class of 2024" (or whatever the graduating year is).
- Create a scholarship committee for every eighth and ninth grader. Put three to four adults on it and make it a mission to help that student go to college. Meet with each student monthly, and ask what his or her interests are. Show students colleges that are a good match for their interests. Share the school coursework they need to take to have the resume for their scholarship application. Line up the tutoring needed so the student gets academic help. Bring all the scholarship forms to the student. Then, sit with him or her to help the student fill out every single form. This whole process is complex and intimidating to students and parents. If you do not help students, it won't happen.
- Bring in guest speakers to share their real-world jobs.
- Read the ebook *40 Alternatives to College* (Altucher, 2012), and share ideas each week.
- Create a schoolwide job fair with students manning the company booths. Each student acts as either a prospective employee or works behind a table, posing as human resources, listing the job requirements, and talking up the company's job openings. Students have to craft a resume and answer questions at the booths.
- Engage the Adopt a College program. For Edenvale Elementary, over three hundred colleges agreed to send free college materials to inspire students. It is the only K–5 school in the country that promises a college scholarship for every high school graduate. Visit http://adopt -a-college.org/about2.html to learn more.

- Ask students to sell their dream to graduate either job ready or college ready to younger students. Fourth or fifth graders can partner up with a buddy and present a career option (like welder or computer programmer) or college to first graders (or twelfth graders to ninth graders). They research and share the job requirements, qualifications, and starting salary. They research similar criteria for college. This will make an impression on all students involved!

Attribute Connections

This fourth strategy is simple but very powerful. Attribute what students are doing now to the probability of a future outcome. Conversely, explain a current outcome based on a prior effect. See figure 10.1. Average teachers miss this key strategy, but high-performing teachers commonly use this gold mine. The effect size, within a specific subject or skill area, is a ridiculously huge 1.42, over two and half years' worth of progress (Dweck, 1999).

Figure 10.1: Attributions help motivate students with repeated cause and effect.

Once students set huge goals for themselves (for example, "I want to become a master electrician" or "I want to start a social media company"), then it's up to you to consistently make the classroom connections between what students do in class and how that helps them reach their goals. Examples include:

- "I love the effort you put in. That same effort is going to help you pass the test to get licensed as an electrician."

- "I loved how you tried many strategies on that problem until you got it. That will help you get the job you want, even if the first five places don't have openings."

- "I like that you refused to give up. That extra effort will help you keep pushing to move up. This effort would help you get a promotion at your new job."

- "Before you began, you thought you could succeed. I bet that positive attitude helped you come through. You'll need that when you start your company you told me about."

- "I love this drawing; it's got great detail and a moving impact. Remember you said you'd like to be an animator someday? This drawing is a huge step toward that. Next, start focusing more on _____. Can you try that?"

These strategies are simple to do and take little effort. These suggestions require little or no willpower on your part or your students'. In fact, sheer willpower has less to do with achievement and more to do with using savvy, tactical strategies to maintain self-control (McGonigal, 2012).

If you don't help students make connections that help them link their actions to the goal they're trying to reach, they will rarely make the connections themselves. This is a critical strategy. When you do make connections, student effort goes up, and you'll build intrinsic motivation because the student sees the connections of the present to their future.

Quick Consolidation

I am hoping I have sold you on the soft skills of achievement. So many teachers try a great strategy in isolation and wonder why it did not produce the effects that they had hoped for. The real reason is that most isolated strategies will fail. But the good news is the effects are cumulative. The more you do, the easier it gets. These will all work dependent on what else is going on. This process of mastering the more hidden or soft side of achievement is critical if you want to foster it. Here we learned that your four primary tools for building a great attitude were your modeling (the achievement mindset and high-achievement thinking), learning to sow the seeds of success, and consistently attributing connections. Each of these has a strong effect, and together they create a synergistic force that almost compels students to achieve more than they thought they ever could.

CHAPTER 11

GIVE FABULOUS FEEDBACK

Every one of the strategies in this book related to student achievement is powerful, but this next one may be the holy grail of generating real student motivation and stronger effort. Here, you get tools to generate better quality feedback. As soon as you and I see progress, we get inspired. With feedback, the goal moves closer, and hope rises. That's how it works for your students too. But hope requires a certain type of feedback. Let's break down the effects of feedback.

Give students intervention feedback on their learning, and get a strong 0.65 effect size (Hattie, 2009), meaning more than one year's worth of academic gains. Give more positives than negatives (3:1 ratio) and be specific enough to focus on key things students can change. Finally, the kinds of high-quality feedback that you'll learn in this chapter have the greatest effect on the weakest learners (Black & Wiliam, 1998). Unfortunately, these types are used the least. But you can change that path. Let's get started with formative assessment.

Ongoing Formative Assessment

Formative feedback measures progress over the long haul. Formative evaluation for both students and teachers has a very high effect size of 0.90 (Hattie, 2009). The term *formative assessment* means you are using the evidence of learning (or lack of it) to adjust instruction toward a goal during the process, not just at the end. (See figure 11.1, page 86, for the feedback loop.) Researchers conclude in one meta-study that regular use of classroom formative assessment raises student achievement by a substantial level—from at least 0.40 to 0.70 standard deviations (Black & Wiliam, 1998).

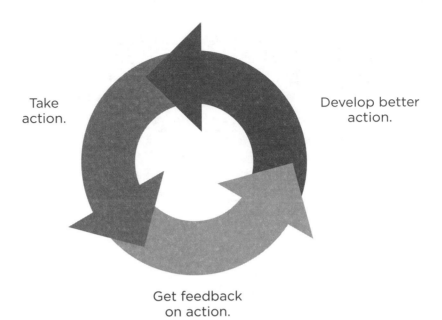

Figure 11.1: Feedback loop.

One of the dangers of teaching without ongoing formative assessment is that you might go a week or two and still be unsure if your students are really "getting it." But if you set up your class for daily multiple checks for understanding, you'll learn fast and adjust fast too. Higher-performing teachers notice quickly what is not working and adjust rapidly, revise, and redo a lesson. Average or struggling teachers may go for a week or two before they figure out what is not working. When that happens over and over, they say, "I just don't have enough time to teach all the content." Actually, they do have time.

In Hattie's (2009) studies, formative assessment is among the top three factors for enhancing student achievement, with an effect size of 0.90. This factor is effective across many variables, including student ages, duration, frequency, and special needs.

No matter what kind of feedback you use in your class, here are the benchmarks with which to measure them. Quality formative assessment needs the following five to work well.

1. **Having clear, shared goals:** Teachers should share with learners specific goals for learning and the criteria for success.
2. **Establishing progress:** Students need to know where they are successful and where you need help.
3. **Providing actionable feedback that moves learning forward:** Students need a way to find out how to get better at what they're doing.

4. **Activating students as owners of their own learning:** Teachers should empower students to engage with the learning alone or collaboratively to grow (learn it, own it, and share it).

5. **Tracking:** Students should see the big-picture trends and the details available.

These feedback benchmarks will lead to far more effective strategies than saying "Nice work" or "Good job." Referring to this list often and posting it near your desk might be the single best way to boost achievement. Also, easy-to-use classroom activities can serve as powerful formative assessments. Here are my three favorites from Robert Marzano's (1998) *A Theory-Based Meta-Analysis of Research on Instruction*.

1. **Relevant recall questions (average effect size of 0.93):** Before you begin a unit, find out what students know and don't know. Use a brief quiz packed with questions designed to bring out useful and essential prior learning into the foundation time. Consider just ten questions, and have students correct their neighbor's paper and turn it in. This gives you a better idea of where to start a unit.

2. **"I Decide, You Decide" (average effect size of 0.89):** Students in pairs alternate deciding and sorting information. Students have the content information on cards, papers, or digital media. You call out the decision to make, and the two students work out the answer. For example in science, you might say, "Compare and contrast oxygen and helium." The students can create a Venn diagram showing the overlap between the two elements, do a mind map, or just make two columns. Then, they share it with the class and get feedback.

3. **Graphic organizers and mind maps (average effect size of 1.24):** Show students an example first and then a blank framework. Sell them on why this is a great way to learn ("It is just like your brain works—it goes from idea to idea to details, then it connects them"). Your students create their own personalized representation of what they are learning and then add illustrations, pictures, or emoticons. Once they are done, they trade organizers with a partner for peer-editing feedback. Then, ask them to turn in their organizers and recreate it from memory. The version they turned into you can be for their final feedback.

This chapter has four more high-performing feedback strategies that draw on the five benchmarks. Our first is qualitative feedback, using the SEA (strategy, effort, and attitude) format. The second is quantitative, using the 3M format for easy recall and application. Third, you'll learn about a simple feedback strategy using index cards. Lastly, you'll gain tools for gathering the most important form of feedback— student feedback.

SEA for Qualitative Feedback

We begin with SEA (strategy, effort, and attitude) because it reinforces critical qualitative attributes that we want to foster in our students over the long haul. Students have no control over their DNA, their parents, or their neighborhood. However, students do have a huge amount of influence over the choices they make (strategy), how hard they work (effort), and the mindset (attitude) they bring to learning. The SEA strategy is a way to reinforce these in the classroom and ask "How am I doing?"

Each of the SEA qualities is a clear and potent replacement for using delayed tests (effect size of 0.31; Hattie, 2009) or saying "Well done" or "Good job" (effect size of 0.09; Kluger & DeNisi, 1996). Instead, using SEA, teachers give specific feedback in regard to strategy, effort, and attitude.

- **Strategy:** "I loved how you kept trying so many *strategies* on that problem until you got it."

- **Effort:** "I like that you refused to give up. That extra *effort* will help you succeed again and reach your goal."

- **Attitude:** "Before you began, you thought you could succeed. Your positive *attitude* helped you come through."

Use the SEA feedback to build drive and long-term effort by changing who, when, and how often you give feedback. The *who* means you should never be the only source of student feedback. The majority should come from the student him- or herself, peers, computers, the physical results of actions, a rubric, or a standard set as a model or a checklist. The *when* means that sooner is better than later. The *how often* might be the most important question of all. Because feedback's contribution to motivation, learning, and achievement is so high, ensure that your students get some kind of feedback (by their peers, the activity itself, reflection, or you) at least once every thirty minutes, every school day of the year. By using specific high-scoring, self-awareness feedback strategies with an effect size of a huge 0.74, you give students the gift of affirmation and light a fire (Marzano, 1998).

SEA is awesome because you can tell your students what they are doing well. Now, let's shift to a more quantitative form of feedback.

3M for Quantitative Feedback

The 3M (milestone, mission, and method) feedback process focuses on orienting students to learning in an empirical way. The beauty of it is its simplicity. This feedback answers the three most essential questions students have about how they are doing: (1) "Where am I at?" (milestone), (2) "Where am I going?" (mission), and (3) "How do I get there?" (method). The effect size is a whopping 1.13, which tells you it is highly effective (Wiliam & Thompson, 2007).

The 3M process involves using feedback with students and training them to use the process, which includes the following three steps.

1. Teach students the 3M process.
2. Ask students to track their progress.
3. Guide students to improvement.

Teach Students the 3M Process

Before students can use the 3M process on their own, you need to first teach them its critical pieces.

- **Milestone (Where am I?):** "Here's where you're at right now. You got eight out of fifteen vocabulary words correct."
- **Mission (What's my goal?):** "Your mission is always to get a 100 percent on the end-of-the-month quiz."
- **Method (How do I get there?):** "You'll need a new strategy and plan to get where you're going. I've posted some ideas you can choose from."

Once you begin to use the 3M process with students, they will see its value. Over time, students will learn to self-assess.

Ask Students to Track Their Progress

For students to self-assess, they need data to track how they are doing. The data are simply their scores, which can come from self-assessments, a returned assignment, a student-graded quiz, or any other form of written, numerical score. So, quality data could be as simple as sixteen out of twenty points on a quiz.

When tracking their data, students should be aware of their mission during this step. The mission is always simple; it is 100 percent. You may have students with special needs who start at a much lower score than the rest of the class. In their case, the mission focus is on 100 percent improvement (from three correct to six correct is a 100 percent improvement). These high expectations are a critical part of the achievement mindset. Do not get swept up into collective agreement from peers who say, "Maybe we should start with something practical, like 70 percent." Keep your gutsy goals high, and focus on the micro goals.

Guide Students to Improvement

A key benefit of the 3M strategy is developing student autonomy. They will quickly figure out their milestone and mission but often need help with their method—how to improve their learning. Post a list of "How I Can Get Better at Learning" tips on the classroom wall to encourage students to try various ways of learning and to figure out, on their own, how they learn best. You can make your own developmentally appropriate list of student learning tools. Here are just a few examples.

- Ask more questions in class.

- Review work, and talk it over.

- Summarize the learning daily.

- Preview learning before class.

- Work closer with a study buddy.

- Create a mind map or graphic organizer of the content.

- Ask the teacher for specific help.

- Look up difficult concepts.

You can also have students draw the list and post it. Imagine the powerful effects when students can take their milestone data (like "Eight of fifteen words correct"), reaffirm their mission ("100 percent on my next vocabulary test"), and decide for themselves how to improve their learning ("Maybe I should ask more questions in class"). See figure 11.2 for a goal tracker students can use to set their milestone, mission, and method.

My Goal Tracker	
Week One	
Milestone	9/15 vocabulary words correct
Mission	15/15 vocabulary words correct
Method	Practice with a partner.
Week Two	
Milestone	12/15 vocabulary words correct
Mission	15/15 vocabulary words correct
Method	Do homework.

Week Three	
Milestone	*14/15 vocabulary words correct*
Mission	*15/15 vocabulary words correct*
Method	*Draw pictures to symbolize words, and self-test.*
Week Four	
Milestone	*15/15 vocabulary words correct*
Mission	*15/15 vocabulary words correct*
Method	*Stay the course and continue.*

Figure 11.2: 3M feedback tracker.

*Visit **go.solution-tree.com/instruction** for a free reproducible version of this figure.*

Students can keep their goal tracker in a folder or digital file, or teachers can post them on the wall as ongoing student work. I love empowering students to know and be able to act on the results of their own learning. They'll know their milestones and their goal (mission), and they'll choose their next step to get better (method). Finally, it's most effective when classrooms use the 3M process at least once or twice a week. To empower your students to become better learners, help them learn the tools to do the work, then connect the dots for them. They need to know how to regulate their own learning. This is the heart of the 3M feedback system.

MIC Feedback

MIC is an acronym for *micro–index card* feedback. It is a fast way to help students get unstuck and move ahead. In many classes, students with less confidence dread taking on challenges, creating, producing, completing, writing papers, or doing projects. One issue they have is starting off on the wrong foot and never quite catching up. MIC feedback deals with that issue. It is a way to get inside a student's head to discover his or her thinking paths (and stuck areas) that might hurt his or her chances for success. In language arts, writing a two-page paper can be overwhelming for students with little writing confidence. In mathematics, doing ten problems is a huge chunk for some students. In science, solving a problem or doing scientific thinking is a challenge. You will notice that the size of the process or project (or the number of steps required) is stressful or overwhelming. But students' approach is key. MIC feedback solves that problem.

How to Gather MIC Feedback

As you start the year (or semester), gathering MIC feedback is simple. Ask students to write their name on the back of an index card. On the other side, ask students to write about one of the following.

- Two things about themselves that you (the teacher) should know but most don't know
- Past experience in the subject area (in five sentences or less)
- How the week has been (what they liked and what they'd change)
- Goals for the class
- About parts of a paper (introduction, theme, thesis, evidence and support, argument rebuttals, summary, and conclusions)
- Three friends in the classroom (to learn how much social glue each student has)
- A five- to ten-word outline of what they are currently working on
- Advice for another, younger, student about how to approach most mathematics problems

For the first two weeks, ask for students to do one of these activities every other day. Read and sort these cards. You will quickly identify which students need which types of differentiation.

How to Use MIC Feedback

With this method, you can learn about specific topics that you would never have time to ask for individually. Over time, students realize they can get help from you (privately, if needed). Initially, this seems like more work. But quickly, students (and you) get the early information correct, and they can move forward in larger chunks faster.

On the social side, you can use the class time to have students work with just the right partner or in a small group to talk about what they put on their card and what they will do next. Soon, students will learn how to support and help each other as they develop empathy and listening skills.

With peer support, students' assignments and projects will fit basic proficiency requirements and then you can focus on moving to mastery levels. Each time you use this process, the students will get just a bit better at using the MIC strategy. Your goal is to develop social and academic competencies faster and earlier so every student can ultimately help another.

Student Feedback

Perhaps surprisingly, the all-time best feedback is student feedback to you, the teacher (Hattie & Timperley, 2007). Getting feedback from students is simple. Consider the following four student feedback strategies.

1. Nonverbal information
2. Yesterday's learning
3. One-minute summary
4. Suggestions box

Nonverbal Information

This is my favorite strategy. It gives you live, real-time information about how you are interacting with your class. You instantly see who is with you and who is not. Start watching for nonverbal information. Observe students during seatwork time. Look for signs of physical or emotional distress during the task so you can stop and ask what your students are experiencing ("Can I check in with you for a moment?"). When you introduce something to your class, watch the body language. If any students roll their eyes and slump back in their seats, that's feedback to you. Your hook or buy-in did not work (or it was missing from your lesson). If everyone except a couple of students is hooked, let each student get started, then go check on the isolated, concerned, or checked-out students. Marzano et al. (2001) describe this use of real-time information as *withitness*, which has a massive effect size of 1.42.

Yesterday's Learning

To find students who are lost, use an activity to get feedback from the previous day's class. Give students a blank sheet of paper and twelve minutes to write down everything they can recall from yesterday's lesson. Then, collect their work and quickly sort it to identify the struggling students. Then, reteach confusing concepts and correct your own teaching mistakes. This way, the students get better and so do you.

One-Minute Summary

You can also use the one-minute summary activity. At the end of class (as an exit pass), ask students to write an anonymous one- to two-minute note on two topics. First, they answer, "What is the most important thing from class today?" Then, your students answer, "What is still a bit confusing to you about today's class?" Even though they're anonymous, which helps students be honest, they'll give you immediate, useful feedback on your teaching.

Suggestions Box

Lastly, instead of having students use your classroom suggestions box in a passive way ("When you feel like it, drop me a suggestion"), use the suggestions box as a feedback tool. You'll ask students before class if they got a bit lost in yesterday's class (and where). Then, during class give everyone a one-minute suggestion moment for feedback. These tools help you collect valuable feedback, especially if you have already taught students how to tell you what they need. At the end of class, use it as an exit pass.

Give students examples and encourage them to be specific with their feedback. Saying "This class sucks" is pretty useless. Ask them to say, "I don't get why we are learning this" and let you know when the lesson doesn't have enough relevance, needs choices, isn't social enough, or is too confusing. Once students know the specific sort of feedback you are looking for, the real magic can start.

After you sort through the suggestions box once a week, tell students what you read, how much you appreciate their responses, and how you'll use their ideas to get better as a teacher. Students are remarkably candid and accurate in their perceptions of classroom climate. Without quality, continuous feedback, you may as well be teaching in a vacuum.

Quick Consolidation

This chapter focused on how students and you can get better with the number-one upgrade tool: feedback. We introduced the power of formative assessment where students are getting feedback (SEA, 3M, and MIC). Then, you learned how students can give you feedback through simple tools.

Savvy teachers use feedback to stay in the know (Marzano & Pickering, 2011). Do you commonly use ongoing formative assessment? If you use the tools in this chapter, you are likely to get pretty good feedback, which informs better teaching. Students cannot control everything that happens to them in class, but through student feedback, they can respond to your teaching. The effect sizes on feedback are very strong. Feedback is the substance for positive change in your work. Seek it out, use it, and enjoy the difference.

CHAPTER 12

PERSIST WITH GRIT

School is not a sprint; it's a marathon. There is a lot of deferred gratification before actually graduating. A portion of students who don't graduate simply give up (versus pursue something perceived as "better"). If you want students to overcome discouragement and failures and succeed in school, they need grit. Some students don't have it. The good news is that you can build this trait.

So when a student's effort drops, it is easy to say, "She's not motivated" or "He doesn't want it very badly." However, you may be confusing self-control with grit. Self-control is the short-term ability to manage attention and effort while avoiding distractions to reach a goal, such as concentrating for a big test. Grit is the tenacity and strength to pursue your long-term goals in the face of obstacles over time, for something worthwhile (Duckworth, Peterson, Matthews, & Kelly, 2007).

It is one of the single most effective traits for student success (Tough, 2012). It is how students deal with adversity and failure and is a greater predictor for student success than IQ (Winerman, 2013). Grit is the pursuit of a longer-term goal (think gutsy goal like getting an advanced degree). In the classroom, a student might have self-control but have very little grit. The opposite can be also true, but in general they go together.

With low self-control and grit, student by student, the collective energy and effort in your classroom drop. This can prompt some teachers to lower their goals and settle for more typical goals of passing or proficiency. However, setting goals for passing or proficiency doesn't challenge students or allow them to grow. The good news is grit and self-control are teachable traits. This chapter will detail strategies to foster grit as a key part of the achievement mindset.

Ten Ways to Develop Grit

Here are ten of the best-researched ways to develop grit, some from an interview with MacArthur Fellowship grantee Angela Duckworth, a pioneer of grit (Winerman, 2013).

1. **Help students continually value their gutsy goal:** Reference student long-term goals in a variety of ways (such as posters, celebrations, micro goals, and stories) so they see the journey as a worthwhile path to the goal. Many times a student will become gritty in a project that is highly personal and meets his or her values. For example, Katie Stagliano felt so badly about hunger among the homeless that at age twelve she founded Katie's Krops (www.katieskrops.com). She grows thousands of pounds of vegetables every year and donates them to the homeless.

2. **Show students what grit looks like:** There are many superb movies that feature grit. Consider scenes in movies such as *Forrest Gump*, *Bend It Like Beckham*, and *Remember the Titans*. But talk about self-control and grit before you show it. Ask students to share something they have already done that shows grit. Most have at least some *partial* grit examples.

3. **Model grit:** Set a gutsy goal for yourself, and share it with the class—for example, learn a new language, run a half-marathon, get a book published, or so on. Then, share the ups and downs with your class as you pursue your own gritty challenge. Your grit may have been completing college or dealing with adversity or an illness. Students need to see, hear, and feel close up what grit is. Many who run a marathon do it not because they love running—it's the friendships, process of getting better, and personal satisfaction of completing a marathon that they're after. Truly gritty people have a history of setting especially challenging long-term goals. If students don't see it, they won't know how to do it.

4. **Teach students the ability to stay in the moment:** Value right now. This focusing tool is more than a bit of Zen because it teaches students to let go of any thoughts about what else they could be doing. A simple deep-breathing activity or quiet reflection activity may start the process for your students. Remember your life is simply a very long sequence of right-now moments. Make each one count.

5. **Create a common grit vocabulary:** Tell students what being gritty is, and what it is not. "Doing that shows me a lot of grit!" Your students need specific ways to identify and describe grit when it occurs. A good starting point is to create a grit baseline. Ask students to stand up and when you say "Go," they run (in place) as hard as they can for thirty seconds. You might have three-fourths of your class slow down before the thirty-second mark. So, your fitness baseline for grit is 25 percent of the class is gritty for running in place.

6. **Assess grit:** You can help your students (middle and high schoolers) assess grit at the start and end of your school year (or semester) using a grit index (see University of Pennsylvania School of Arts and Sciences, 2011). Visit **go.solution-tree.com/instruction** to access a direct link to this grit index. Consider revising this index for your elementary students as well.

7. **Foster conditions for grit:** Build classroom positivity through celebrations, smiles, upbeat music, and affirmations. Positive emotions like optimism tell students that the future is good and it is worth working toward a big goal. You get maximum value in resilience and grit building when the ratio of positives to negatives is about 3:1 (Catalino & Fredrickson, 2011). Ensure that every student before he or she goes home has gotten much more positives (affirmations, quality feedback, nonverbal encouragement, and so on) than negatives (criticism, negative nonverbals, exclusion, and so on).

8. **Make grit real in many ways:** Use metaphors, quotes, and analogies to refer to grit so students understand it and know exactly what it is. Tell your students that they may not be responsible for getting knocked down, but they are responsible for getting back up. Jamie, our teacher in New Orleans, uses two objects to highlight what grit is. One is a real egg, and the other is a special bouncy ball—a Super Ball. The question he asks is, "Are you an egg or a Super Ball?" For a demonstration, he drops both the egg and Super Ball on the floor. The egg breaks, but the Super Ball bounces back stronger than before. Then, the class participates in a choral recall again and again. "Which one are you?" Students say, "Super Ball. "I didn't hear you!" the teacher says. "One more time?" Finally, the class roars, "SUPER BALL!"

9. **Reinforce grit in action:** Every time you see a student pushing through obstacles, say, "Love the way you're being so gritty with that task." When a student gets frustrated, do not make excuses ("I understand that not everyone succeeds" or "Maybe this is not your thing"). Affirm students' strengths and give them a pep talk on how you are all in this for the long haul and that this was just a glitch and a time to adapt. They need to know you're on their side.

10. **Give grit a chance:** If everything you do over the course of a semester can be done in a few seconds, minutes, or hours, students will never get a chance to develop grit. In arts, students learn to perfect a skill over a period of months or years. In sports, grit develops over the course of a season. You'll need to create opportunities for students to develop tenacity over the long term with at least one project. The team (or partner) project should take months to complete (students might work on it weekly). For example, students might write a twelve-page guide for success to give next year's students that illustrates what they've learned over the course of a semester or year.

Keep your perspective developmental. For a first grader, grit might mean sticking with something for a week or even a day. Students can start the year with small, twenty-minute activities, but remember the power of asking. Ask for great things out of your students. Students won't do what you don't expect or ask them to do. After a short time, they're ready for something that takes some work every day over two weeks. Soon, and as students mature, you'll be ready to offer projects that take weeks or months.

Additionally, when students are negative or disappoint you, you're getting a gift to develop new skills. Show them how to deal with frustration and disappointment. However, do not let yourself get negative in your efforts trying to reinforce the power of positivity. Instead, stay calm. Foster strengths, and give feedback and support. Say, "I'm glad you see where you're at; that's always a good start. Now, let's recheck where we're going so we can figure out our next step to fill the gap. Once we've done that, I'll ask you for your plan, and I'll also ask if you need any extra support."

Tools for When Grit Drops

All of us have had lapses in our grittiness. Researchers have uncovered strategies that reignite the passion to get the grit back in action. When grit drops, connect their values and identity to the task to infuse new energy and effort for success (Cohen, Garcia, Purdie-Vaughns, Apfel, & Brzustoski, 2009). Here are several ways to do this.

Ask students to take a five-minute break. For the first two minutes, students are given a stretch, deep-breathing activities, or a faster energizer. For the next three minutes, ask students to sit and write down a list of their qualities or personal characteristics. Their list might include honesty, humor, and loyalty. Once they think they are finished, ask them to think a bit and add some more. The truth is, all of us have dozens of character traits. The beauty of this list is that it allows the student to see right there in front of him or her "Who am I?" It usually fosters more grittiness.

I've had success in similar situations by reframing the class and adopting the expert-in-training identity. For example, a student who is poor in mathematics wouldn't hang in there for twenty minutes trying to solve a problem. However, an expert in training *would* hang in there for twenty minutes.

Many successful teachers call their students *scholars*. The label is critical when you want to build character traits such as grit. Say to students, "In the past, a few of you might not have stuck with this task. But you're scholars now. Mistakes are our friend, and as an expert in training, you realize it takes time to get good." Encouraging posters (like Working Harder Gets You Smarter) can help foster grit.

Finally, encourage students to use the following simple three-step strategy to deal with grit breakdowns.

- **Step 1: Listen**—When you're about to take on a task or a big challenge, listen to your self-talk. Listen for any sign of the fixed mindset. What does it say in your head? Is it a voice that limits you? If it is, switch to the growth mindset voice, which says, "I am not defined by my past or my mistakes. I can learn and solve this problem no matter what it takes."

- **Step 2: Reactivate**—What's the goal that you have, and why is it important for you to achieve it? Activate a clear, sensory-rich image and sound of the goal you want. See it, hear it, and feel the joy of accomplishing your goal right in the moment. Tell a partner why it is important to reach the goal. Next, share how you (or those you help) will feel when you reach the goal.

- **Step 3: Choose again**—Remember that it's your own brain and your own voice, and you're not a robot. What's the new achievement mindset that will best help you get your goal? If your voice says, "I don't think I can do this. It's a huge job, and I'm not sure how to do it. I'm afraid I'll fail" choose an alternative. Change the predictive self-talk. Talk to yourself and say, "I have succeeded at many things before when I was unsure at the start. If I need help, I'll ask for it. When I make mistakes, I'll learn from them. My goal is important and nothing worthwhile is easy. I'm ready!"

When it comes to maintaining goals, constantly reactivate students' grit so they remember why they wanted to reach their goals. Over the course of days, weeks, and months, your students' enthusiasm will go up and down. Your role is to find a variety of ways to make the same gutsy goal interesting. For example:

- Ask students to find a YouTube clip that conveys the message of their goal.

- Ask students to prepare a thirty-second presentation to the class on their gutsy goal, and why they'll reach it.

- Have students show their goal tracker depicting where they started, where they are now, and what they have to do next to reach their goal.

- Have students stand, walk ten seconds, find a partner, and share with their new partner their goals, obstacles, and methods for overcoming setbacks.

This type of variation helps students' goals feel real. Students are able to validate their goals with other students and internalize them as they present.

Quick Consolidation

To foster grit, you were introduced to ten strategies. Every one of these can help, but start using three, four, or more of these, and your class grit will rise like a hot-air balloon. Yes, grit is important. You can build grit. And it's free and fairly easy to do it. For the moment, take in what you have so far. You have plenty to start making some miracles.

If you are going to inspire a dream, you'll want to provide the resources to make it happen. Now we are starting to see what it takes. We began with relationships, and then moved to the achievement mindset. That included setting goals, having the right attitude, giving fabulous feedback, and persisting with grit.

CHAPTER 13

LOCK IN THE ACHIEVEMENT MINDSET

If you have had a tough time motivating students to do their best, there's usually a story in your head that explains why those students underperform. Maybe you are thinking, "Of course students from low-income families are more lazy; look at their home lives!" However, according to the Economic Policy Institute (Boushey, Bernstein, & Mishel, 2002), poor working adults actually spend more hours working each week than their wealthier counterparts.

In addition, the shortage of living-wage jobs that need only a high school education (like factory jobs) means that many poor adults work multiple jobs. Poor people, on average, have the same work ethics and levels of motivation as wealthier people (Iversen & Farber, 1996; Wilson, 1997). While some stereotype the poor as lazy, over three-fourths of children from low-income families have at least one employed parent, and two-thirds have at least one parent who works full-time year round (Douglas-Hall & Chau, 2007). So, if socioeconomic status is not the answer for why students are failing, what is? Hold up a mirror.

If students have acted lazy and unmotivated in your classes, year after year, you have two choices. One is to blame the students. That gets you off the hook for any accountability. You can just say, "Those students are not cut out for academics." But your own personal experiences are a grain of sand in the universe of big data. There are thousands of high-performing teachers who work in high-poverty schools. Also, remember, it was you who was the only common denominator; the students change every year. Don't draw conclusions and judgments about students before you hold up a mirror. Ask yourself, "Do you have the achievement mindset? Are you instilling students with the achievement mindset?" Let's revisit a teacher with the achievement mindset.

In previous chapters, I mentioned Jamie, a secondary mathematics teacher who challenges students to achieve and motivates them to learn a subject that most dislike. To sell students on doing something greater, he uses almost every achievement mindset strategy. When he uses these strategies, students know it's not just about getting a good test score; it's about changing the future—their future.

Let's walk though again how he puts these in the classroom. First and foremost, he's passionate about New Orleans Saints football, so he uses a football theme to hook students (see Arakaki, 2010). He keeps students engaged, challenges them, and celebrates often. He creates multiple challenging goals for students and provides detailed feedback.

- **Goals:**
    - He encourages students to crush Lusher's test scores, a nearby affluent school.
    - Students work to beat mathematics scores on a college entrance exam to get a scholarship.
- **The right attitude:**
    - He models the achievement mindset and thinking by breaking the bonds of mediocrity, giving students a chance at big-time status.
    - He sells his students that reaching the goals are not only possible but a mission, a mandate, and even their destiny.
    - He offers a can of soda as a tangible reward when students collaborate, participate, or complete their homework.
    - He makes explicit connections between perfect homework, his class values, and the two gutsy goals, so students realize small choices and victories do matter.
- **Fabulous feedback:**
    - He uses the Heisman Hopefuls bulletin board and posts successful student assessments as All-American, All-State, and All-City. The posting allows students to see where they stand among their peers.

- He is careful about who he calls on, ensuring everyone gets attention and feedback on his or her contributions.
- Students fill out graphic organizers with class data and share. A student might say, "I got a Basic on the quiz, but I need to get a Mastery next time. My plan is to ask way more questions in class."

- **Grit:**

  - He uses the powerful metaphor and demonstration "Are you a Super Ball or an egg?"
  - He uses constant pep talks when effort sags. He shows students that he knows they can do well and constantly encourages them.

If you ever think your students just "don't have it," go back and review this high-performing teacher's strategies. You'll see what it takes to turn your students into a gushing success that you want to brag about!

Change the Narrative, Change Your Teaching

The last few chapters have been about building an achievement mindset. If you feel achievement is all up to genes, the neighborhood, or parenting, you have no chance to become a high-performing teacher. Yes, those factors do matter; but you matter even more. There is no inherited work ethic. We learn it from our families, outside role models, peers, and teachers. There are rich people who are lazy. There are middle-class people who are lazy. There are poor people who are lazy. Remember, socioeconomic status doesn't establish laziness; life experiences do. If you want greater student achievement, change the student's experience at school.

You can do this. You can help your students succeed. If you point fingers at others, you won't grow. If you struggle with test scores, behaviors, graduation, student engagement, and attendance, it may be a good time for changes. Strong teachers change their students' mindsets about learning, school, and success. As soon as you decide that you have a choice, you realize that you can alter your life story and each student's story. Here's a powerful narrative for you: when you change, your students will change. This achievement narrative combines the attitudes, beliefs, and stories about why students achieve. If you grasp how strong achievement comes from teachable goals, attitudes, feedback, and grit, then you have the power to make amazing changes. What mindset narrative do you have? See figure 13.1 (page 104).

You Are Your Mindset: Which Is Yours?

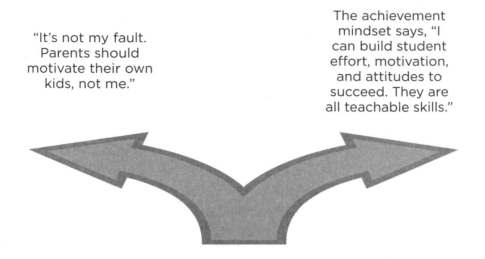

"It's not my fault. Parents should motivate their own kids, not me."

The achievement mindset says, "I can build student effort, motivation, and attitudes to succeed. They are all teachable skills."

Figure 13.1: You are your mindset—the achievement mindset.

Fill in the following blanks with your name and a strategy from this mindset. Repeat the phrase daily until it's automatic.

"I, _____, am committing to developing the achievement mindset in my students every single day. I will begin with one of the strategies mentioned, which is _____. I will continue this until I have mastery and it's automatic. At that point, I'll learn something new to foster student success."

Reflection and Decision

You have seen by now that meaningful and lasting change starts with a mirror. Self-assess first. Are effort and achievement issues in your class? Remember, you always have a choice: do you want students to graduate job or college ready, or do you want to make excuses for why they failed? Your decision to grow students in a more self-confident, achievement-minded mindset includes a new narrative about yourself and your students, achievement boosters to develop the mindset with a fierce urgency, and a support process to ensure successful implementation. That support process may involve colleagues, websites (like 10 Minute Lesson Plans, http://10minutelessonplans.com), notes to oneself, and new strategies and narratives. If you're ready to rock, you now have the tools to help you begin.

Quick Consolidation

Thousands of teachers have already successfully motivated students from disadvantaged backgrounds. You can do it too. Your own mindset is a critical piece of the puzzle. Before you ever, *ever* claim that a student is unmotivated, ask yourself if you have carefully developed the achievement mindset using this part's tools. There are no unmotivated students, only students in unmotivated classrooms. Let's make some magic happen. Collect the tools you have and make a plan.

PART THREE

WHY THE RICH CLASSROOM CLIMATE MINDSET?

CHAPTER 14

SECRETS OF THE RICH CLASSROOM CLIMATE MINDSET

The title of this mindset plays off the word *rich* in the book's title. Similarly, the word *rich* refers to substantial, bountiful, ample, and plentiful. This metaphor is important because your classroom climate must be rich in affirmation, rich in relevancy, rich in engagement, and rich in relationships. The richness that you share with your students must feel like the good life. And, you'll learn how to do that in the next few chapters. This short chapter focuses on the claim that a rich climate is worth your time and the evidence to support that claim.

I remember very clearly two different middle school teachers. I have vivid memories of working harder for those teachers than I had for any other teachers. It was as if there was a supercharged motor inside me, and I almost couldn't stop myself. I just kept reading, writing, and doing extra credit for both of them, until one teacher actually said to me, "That's enough!"

As you might guess, this was an unusual behavior for me. My grades in middle school were not good, and most teachers called me a behavior problem and a slacker. What on earth got me so fired up to work my tail off for those teachers? The class subject? The content? The teacher? I liked the subjects and teachers, but what really turned me into a high performer was the class culture. Those two teachers were really good at creating a class culture that fostered student achievement. There was camaraderie, competition, and curiosity seemingly every day. What this personal experience showed me is that the same student who is, by all accounts, acting lazy in one teacher's class environment, may actually become a highly motivated learner in another teacher's class.

You see, classroom climate is no accident. Teachers who have great climates for learning are quite purposeful.

This part shows you how much class climate really matters and highlights real teachers who teach students from poverty. Our goal is to foster a rich (or abundant, substantial, unrestricted, and bountiful) classroom climate that meets all students' needs. In a rich classroom climate, students feel comfortable and safe enough to take academic and behavioral risks. It inspires students to dream big. Most of all, it gives students a voice, and it respects them. A climate comprised of energy, participation, spirit, respect, learning, movement, listening, sharing, reflection, and big goals ultimately creates a high-performing classroom.

People often use the terms *climate* and *culture* interchangeably. However, there is a clear difference between the two. Culture is *what* we do (behaviors and character), but climate is *how* we feel. Culture establishes and predicts behaviors ("Who are we?"), but climate follows the crowd and the mood of the moment and is an aggregate of student states. To change culture, we must make decisions and actions that foster our collective culture. Culture takes purpose to change; climate can change in moments. See table 14.1.

Table 14.1: Class Culture Versus Class Climate

Class Culture	Class Climate
Develops values and collective beliefs over time	Develops within seconds or minutes individually
Fosters student decision making	May come or go without consistency
Uses peer pressure and camaraderie to influence more appropriate actions	Characterizes an instant collective emotional feel of the classroom

Make your culture welcoming for every student (not your favorites or those on time every day). A culture should invite reflection on how our behaviors affect us, others, and our school and develop shared beliefs that we are a part of something special and great. Build your culture to foster language that facilitates personal pride, purpose, and energy. Repeat key positive words and phrases, and ensure optimal conditions for learning are ever-present.

Alternatively, your classroom climate influences student behaviors, and the collective behaviors demonstrate classroom culture. You influence the climate to develop the culture you want. Group expectations, rules, and behaviors compose culture. Environments shape our experiences, and those experiences foster our predictions, which change our behaviors (Kirsch, 1999). In the same way that water surrounds fish, culture shapes students' perspectives and develops courses of action, and climate is the vehicle to changing culture. Changing students' attitudes about school (climate) is influential in changing culture. That's why to most students, the classroom climate is the most important thing about school.

The Rich Classroom Climate Mindset

Let's distinguish between a rich classroom climate mindset and a more random classroom climate mindset. Some teachers may ignore the class climate. However, when your students come to you stressed or unprepared for the grade level or subject matter, it is easy to make students the cause of your problems. Teachers with the wrong mindset often do that. In their minds, students should already know how to behave, how to form and maintain teams, how to ask appropriate questions, how to persist in the face of adversity, and how to learn tough concepts with no help. The rich classroom climate mindset says, "I focus on what students need to succeed and build it into the learning and social environment every day." This mindset is critical to understanding your students.

> The rich classroom climate mindset says, "I focus on what students need to succeed and build it into the learning and social environment every day."

When students fail to perform at high levels, some teachers say, "Well, what do you expect?" Those teachers typically think building a rich classroom climate is a waste of time. Do you recognize these comments?

- "My job is teaching content. If students don't want to learn it, that's their loss. They need to sit up and knock off the silly stuff."

- "I don't know what's wrong with him. He's been a piece of work since day one."

- "Students want class to be all fun and warm fuzzies? Tell them to wake up and get with the real world. Class is for learning; it's not supposed to make every kid happy!"

Your goal as a teacher is to create a classroom culture that encourages students to come to school on time, fully prepared, and willing to develop the high self-regulatory skills, grit, and relationships in class. It's not easy. However, if you want to succeed with students from poverty, you'll need to bring your A-game to class every day. That means you'll need the rich classroom climate mindset, the core strategies to back it up, and a will to win this battle.

Let's assume you want a successful class of high-performing students, many of whom likely grew up in poverty. Fortunately, many teachers already have found the solution. Here are their comments.

- "My class will always have a safe place to learn and students who listen to each other. Students also know they can trust me and that I'll give them a fair shake and respect."

- "Students know my class is a great place to grow. They have a voice, goals, and dreams. They can be themselves, make mistakes, and take academic risks, and I'll always be on their side."

- "My students know I will do everything in my power to help them succeed. They know we all will make mistakes. But none of us will fail. They know they have to work hard and play fair. But I have promised them, when they do that, they'll graduate."

These teachers consider their classroom to be a sanctuary from the common stressors of home-life stress, and they create an inviting, respectful place to learn every day. The students feel it, and they, in turn, come to learn by bringing their best effort every day. It's a partnership that is beautiful to behold. One of the two biggest differences between low- and high-performing teachers is that the high performers build a positive school and classroom climate (Jensen, 2014). Is your classroom climate over-the-top good?

A Hard Look at the Evidence

Some believe that class climate is an aggregate of everything, including relationship formation, instruction, cooperative learning, discipline strategies, curriculum, expectations, and engagement. That's why it's so valuable. High-performing teachers say, "*How* do I affirm what's good and make up any differences?" They work hard at it every day. That's why the individual teacher's classroom climate has a powerful 0.80 effect size (Hattie, 2009). This is almost two years' worth of academic gains. See figure 14.1.

Using a rich classroom climate to form a rich classroom culture is never an accident. It's a process, built through a complex, and often subtle, array of social, emotional, and academic strategies, including the process of daily positive comments, experiences, and activities that slowly ramp up classroom energy and confidence. Additionally, a positive school climate predicts student achievement at high-poverty schools. In a study of ten high-poverty schools (with 75 percent or greater free and reduced meals), half were high performers (in the top 25 percent academically in the state) and half were low (bottom 25 percent). The teachers who fostered a positive classroom and school climate were over four times more likely to be at a high-performing school (Jensen, 2014).

Compare and Contrast: Two Classroom Climates

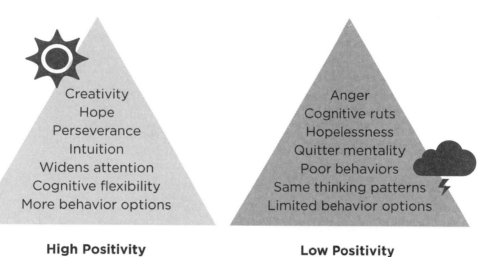

Figure 14.1: High positivity versus low positivity.

Hope and optimism-building climate are also powerful in generating greater student achievement (Rand, 2009). Managing student stress levels in your classroom is critical because students from poverty typically experience chronic stress, which impairs cognitive flexibility, behavioral change, working memory, and thinking skills (Heckman, 2006). Be purposeful in managing the emotional climate. Research suggests that the classroom's emotional climate strongly correlates with the level of academic achievement (Reyes, Brackett, Rivers, White, & Salovey, 2012).

Studies show that teacher effectiveness is a major determinant of student academic progress (Hattie, 2009; Petty, 2009). When you augment classroom climate and the effect size for teacher effectiveness (a robust 0.98), you have a powerful combination (Wenglinsky, 2002). Now that you're (hopefully) sold on the potency of climate, let's explore what makes it work.

Quick Consolidation

The rich classroom climate mindset is simple. Focus on what students need to succeed, and build that environment every day. Remember that relationships are first. Your students want to know, "Should I invest any energy in you (the teacher) or the curriculum, the learning, or my classmates? It's up to you (the teacher) to make my investment currency worthwhile."

Each of the following factors strengthens a different area of students' lives. If you don't purposefully invest thoughtfulness and clear positive actions into your classroom climate, your job can become a nightmare every day. It will be filled with tardy students with motivation and discipline issues who act out, roll their eyes, and make comments behind your back. But my promise is simple: developing a rich classroom climate mindset will transform your classroom into one amazing place to learn, and you'll love your job every day. Next, we'll explore the following three factors that promote a rich classroom climate mindset.

1. Engage voice and vision.

2. Set safe classroom norms.

3. Foster academic optimism.

Take a moment, and reflect on your own practice. What are you currently doing to foster these three items? How much or how often do you foster them? How successful are you? These are important thoughts to take into the upcoming three chapters.

CHAPTER 15

ENGAGE VOICE AND VISION

The first step in creating a rich classroom climate mindset means creating a positive, responsive environment. We focus on what students need to succeed and build it into the learning and social environment every day. That means showing students who they are, what they care about, and how they feel about things. Otherwise, students will feel like it's "your class" and not "our class."

This chapter touches on three elements that make all the difference to students: (1) relevance, (2) student voice, and (3) and student vision. Let's start with relevance.

Relevance

Your students want to know "What's in it for me?" Relevance is everything to your students. If their brain does not buy into classroom learning, it is not changing (Green & Bavelier, 2008). If the brain doesn't change, no learning will occur (Engineer et al., 2012). If no learning happens, why should students even come to school? Chapter 21 will also address relevance in regard to buy-in, but here, we'll touch on its importance for a rich classroom climate. Relevance answers the question "Why should I learn this?" for students. You can either be a teacher who expects students to make all the relevancy connections or builds relevancy into class. Students feel respected when teachers understand where they are coming from and apply that understanding by making connections in the classroom. Create a student's sense of meaning and belonging. Then, show respect for the student's history and culture by engaging his or her voice and vision. The connections will foster brain change and help answer the student's question, "Does my teacher even know who I am or care?" In other words, do you connect the content to students' lives?

An important way to answer the questions "What's in it for me?" and "Why should I even learn this?" is relating to students' culture. Cultural relevance is when students are able to relate course content to their own culture and the context in which they live it. Students wonder if you know where they're coming from (Gay, 2010).

In a nutshell, ask yourself the following four questions to foster a great classroom environment. These four areas have to be rock solid or you'll risk losing students who fail to see you and the content as a relevant part of their learning experience.

1. **Are you affirming?** Culturally relevant teaching is validating and affirming because it acknowledges the strengths of students' diverse heritages.

    Teachers who create a rich classroom climate advocate for students sharing their own personal experiences with their classmates and understand and verbally validate the need for students to operate in their two worlds: home community and school. When a student shares something from his or her home or neighborhood, say, "Thank you; I am glad you shared that with all of us. It's important for us to learn about each other."

2. **Is your teaching diverse?** Culturally relevant teaching is comprehensive. It uses culturally familiar resources to teach knowledge, skills, values, and attitudes through the classroom environment, teaching methods, and even evaluation.

    Utilize a diverse curriculum with content showing faces just like your students' (Gollnick & Chinn, 2013). Use text that shares your students' cultural point of view. Use reciprocal teaching, where students and teachers take turns leading and teaching a subunit in class. Use cooperative learning where each student has a role to play and takes turn in contributing.

3. **Are you empowering?** Culturally relevant teaching empowers students, giving them opportunities to excel in the classroom and beyond: "Empowerment translates into academic competence, personal confidence, courage, and the will to act" (Gay, 2010, p. 34).

    Expose students to strong role models from their own culture as well as those from other cultures (Gonzalez-Mena & Pulido-Tobiassen, 1999). Do you provide opportunities for students to have leadership roles in class? Do you bring in guests who match the ethnicity of your class?

4. **Are you life changing?** Culturally relevant teaching is transformative because educators and their students must often defy educational traditions and the status quo.

    Do you help guide students though the scholarship process? Do you help them learn how to get jobs? Do you help them get tutoring so they can take the tough classes in high school? Or do you sit back and wonder why "they" are so lazy? If you don't help them, the cycle of poverty will continue. Consider using Advancement Via Individual Determination (AVID). AVID is a program originally from the San Diego, California, public schools that helps underrepresented students (including those from different cultural groups) by mixing low-achieving students with high-achieving students in college-preparation programs.

Culturally responsive teachers get to know, respect, and care for every single learner by holding sky-high expectations, ensuring rigor in the curriculum, and providing every type of support needed for students to meet those high expectations (Banks et al., 2005). These teachers have purposefully reflected on their own biases and have discovered how their attitudes can and do shape students' behaviors. As a result, they make it a habit to avoid any racist and discriminatory words or actions (Gay, 2010). If this seems like taking a class in a foreign language, it might be one. All I can say is, "If the shoe fits, wear it."

Student Voice

Student voice is the right-now expression of feelings, opinions, and narratives. When students have a voice in class, they feel heard and validated. This strengthens self-confidence in learning because they now are able to stoke the fire. Help students find their voices so that it makes the task personal, meaningful, and relevant. Then, validate their voices, always affirming and gently sharing the difference between facts and opinions. Say, "I love that you shared your opinion with us. Hope to hear from you again tomorrow."

Having a voice and being listened to are essential human needs. Humans have expressed their voice through cave art, gestures, writing, art, voting, music, and action groups. Voice gives all of us a feeling of being important, appreciated, honored, and respected. When there is a march in Washington, DC, protestors share their voice. With a voice, your students will feel more in control because there is a choice of their input and more of their heart and soul in the class. The class becomes *our class* instead of only the teacher's class. It is critically important to all students to be heard. See figure 15.1 (page 118).

Students feel:

- Heard
- Validated
- Affirmed
- Worthwhile

Results in:

- Feeling more included
- Willingness to work hard
- Gains in self-confidence

Figure 15.1: The power of student voice.

In the We All Have a Voice program (http://weallhaveavoice.org), New Mexico teacher Melinda Forward helps students organize powerful projects to help high-poverty students get their voices heard. All students have dreams, but their personal history will certainly shape, embolden, or even restrain them. Drawing inspiration from Candy Chang's (http://candychang.com) civic engagement projects, Melinda asked students to make a list of five things they'd like to do before they die (see figure 15.2). It was a huge school-wide hit. Students filled up a wall of a building with their chalk dreams (M. Forward, personal communication, May 15, 2015).

Source: Used with permission from Melinda Forward and Kristen Victorino.

Figure 15.2: "Before I die" chalk dreams.

The results from the We All Have a Voice program are far greater participation and engagement with a stronger, more unified school culture.

Consider the following opportunities for inspiring student voice.

- **Invite students to share needs:** Ask questions, meet their learning style, seek help, advocate for academic success tools (like tutoring), use a suggestions box, and stand up for rights (such as gender, sexual orientation, ethnic, or religious).

- **Validate and use student *currencies*:** Understand their tacit knowledge, soft skills, social skills, and network affiliation (R. Jackson, 2011).

- **Invite students to share personal issues with a safe adult:** Encourage them to talk to a teacher, counselor, or anyone who respects privacy and listens well.

- **Encourage students to take risks:** They can challenge their school to change, run for office, create a social media presence, utilize clubs, and undertake school issues and community problems that need attention.

- **Invite students to make allies in life:** Show students why and how adults can be helpful, help them communicate better with their parents, and learn from what doesn't work well.

- **Inspire students to write and speak publicly:** Their voice can only be heard if they share it; help them get exposure to others who want to hear them.

Additionally, when students use their voice, affirm their dreams, opinions, stories, expressions, interests, and life experiences. Consider the following responses, and modify them as necessary.

- "I'm glad we were able to talk. How you feel is important to me."
- "I love your dream; let's see what we can do to make it happen."
- "Thanks for telling your story; I really liked hearing from you."
- "Wow, that was really something. Thanks."
- "In this assignment, write about what you care about using your *I* voice."
- "Good to hear from you; your story was well worth hearing, and I thank you."
- "I love the excitement in your answer. How did you come up with it?"
- "I'm glad you're thinking this through."

- "You also sound a bit hesitant and unsure. Tell us what your concerns are about the answer?"

- "You started off well. Tell me a bit more."

- "I love hearing from you. I'd love to hear from you again. Can you give it a try soon?"

When you give students the opportunity to share their voice and you affirm it, you have given them one of the great gifts that anyone can give another human being. You are saying, "You're important to me and worth listening to."

Student Culture and History

Each student's voice is an expression of his or her identity. Teachers who help students develop their ethnic, cultural, or racial identity unlock a key piece for student success. Racial and ethnic identity, for African American and Latino students especially, is a positive asset (not an adverse one) toward outcomes. In fact, the research shows that during early adolescence, there are consistent, normative, and productive identity explorations and identifications. Cultivation of pride in and identification with youths' racial-ethnic groups was associated with positive adjustment and development (Quintana, 2007). This must be negotiated independent from their parents as they reach puberty. This is critical because African American and Latino students deal with and must resolve two ethnic identity conflicts: (1) dealing with racial biases toward themselves and their group and (2) confronting norms of their own culture and mainstream society (Phinney, Lochner, & Murphy, 1990). Without helping them deal with these issues, you'll see students who struggle. When you help students resolve their own identity by discovering their voice, you empower your students. Being black or Hispanic is critical to defining their psychological well-being (Caldwell, Zimmerman, Bernat, Sellers, & Notaro, 2002), yet many teachers dismiss these identities and have subtle or blatant racial biases in the classroom (Boykin, Tyler, Watkins-Lewis, & Kizzie, 2006). In a study on resilience, the negative effects of racial bias were reduced when African American students felt that being black was good and essential to their identity (Sellers, Caldwell, Schmeelk-Cone, & Zimmerman, 2003).

You have to be able to appreciate, respect, and understand your students' culture to hook them in. Students feel it when you're authentic and show you care about their lives. This is so critical when teaching students of a different ethnicity and socioeconomic status than your own. When you consider and implement cultural factors into daily classroom experiences, you reduce the separation between what students refer to as the real world and the artificial school experience. Researchers studying underachievement among African American students found that real-world connections led to increased motivation and achievement (Butler-Barnes, Williams, & Chavous, 2012). Consider the following example.

Student Culture and History: An Example

In Chicago, a middle school history teacher, Katy Lyons, shows her students that history is never finished and helps them locate their own lives and issues within current events (Lyons, 2012). She takes her students to the Chicago History Museum and lets them find the connections to their areas of interest. For over 95 percent of her students, this is the first time they have ever been to this museum, so they're in awe. Some students lock into the Social Activism Gallery, while others find different areas of fascination. Her students reflect on their own lives, and they narrow down the personal issues at the museum that they find most relevant. Their issues may include peer pressure, neighborhood violence, or social justice. As students investigate these issues, the connections get stronger, and their interest in the subject area deepens. Getting students to research and write about relevant history to each student's life is easy, the teacher says.

She introduces accountability to students so they know their voice and vision are important. Each student publicly presents his or her work to an audience of peers and judges at the schoolwide history fair. She offers her students many different ways to connect to the content, validating their voices from the very beginning of the semester. Once she has hooked their interest and relevance, she puts stakes in the game so that they care about learning because it includes them. Her students work hard on something that they care about and, as a result, their academic scores are strong.

Student Vision

Vision is the student's expectation about his or her own future. We learned earlier that a student's expectation of success has a powerful 1.44 effect size (Hattie, 2009). An empowering expectation affirms having a sense of creative decision making and control over one's destiny. It means everything to students, especially students who come from adversity. It also means a lot for those who don't come from poverty. When you allow a student's positive vision to be embedded in his or her time at school, school feels different, like the student owns it.

In chapter 9, you learned about setting gutsy goals. That process is a teacher-facilitated process to help students pick an *academic* milestone to become more focused. In this case, helping a student find or uncover his or her vision is different. With a student's vision, we are all about discovering and allowing the students' big idea to emerge. A student's vision is about his or her personal life. The teacher's goal here is to ensure that the two (gutsy goals and vision) match up. Sometimes that is easy, and other times it is a bit of work. Here are three ways to uncover or discover your students' visions.

1. **Start with asking students for their long-term dreams (their vision):** The vision often begins with a fuzzy ideal. Those who don't already have one may benefit from hearing others' dreams. You can find these online. Google the

phrase "teens or students who have changed the world" to get ideas. Some stellar examples are Zhan Haite (a fifteen-year-old Chinese political activist), Jordan Romero (the youngest person to ever climb Mount Everest—at thirteen), and Kelvin Doe (a seventeen-year-old self-taught West African engineer who is the youngest visiting practitioner at the Massachusetts Institute of Technology; Edcoogle, 2014; Kaiman, Holpuch, Smith, Watts, & Topping, 2013). Typically, teens with big goals will need some help to flesh them out and define them. When you ask students for their goals or dreams, remember to be receptive, not judgmental. ("Tell me what you have so far, you can edit it later.") Give opportunities for students to write about their dreams, share them ("Share what you have with your partner, if you're comfortable doing that"), and work toward reaching them ("Let's sort out the steps you need to reach your goals").

2. **Help students refine their dreams by using the revised SMART (specific and strategic, measurable, amazing, relevant, and time bound) goals criteria:** Ask students to explain what the end result would look like, sound like, and feel like. Over time, you can help them crystallize this vision into a clear endpoint that they can describe and measure. For students with a vision, they now have an endpoint worth striving for. Now, you can work with students to set micro goals to move them toward their dreams.

3. **Set the goals:** Ask students to use a tablet, laptop, or flipchart paper to create a timeline. Put *Start* at one end and *Goal* at the other end. This process is ideally done with a partner. Allow students to start filling in the milestones they would need to reach in order to accomplish their life vision. Once the smaller milestones are filled in, ask them to work backward all the way to the start. Do they need to get a good grade in your class? Usually they do. That's a great start. One student might have a life goal to become president, the micro goal would be to pass the class she is in now, and her short-term goal would be to graduate from high school. Another student's weekly goal might be to get a B in his or her English class in order to achieve his life goal to write a bestselling book. Notice how the vision may blend into the student's gutsy goals. It all starts with building skills in school. With your motivation, students will feel inspired about their potential destination.

Once students have a vision and a dream for themselves, help them get used to the end result. Ask students to show you the end product. Get students out of their seats, and ask them to stand. Here you should play songs like the theme from *Rocky* ("Gonna Fly Now") or "Unbelievable" by EMF. With the music playing, ask students (while standing) to physically rehearse success poses like graduating, getting an award, getting the job they want, winning a game, getting a medal in the Olympics, or winning a championship.

Have students show three different success poses and then jump into a tough new task. These simple routines change the brain's chemistry, as demonstrating high-power poses influence elevations in testosterone, decreases in cortisol (stress), and increased feelings of power and tolerance for risk (Carney, Cuddy, & Yap, 2010). These changes can support better learning and are powerful for celebration.

Quick Consolidation

You were introduced to the relevance of cultural responsiveness, student voice, and student vision. These are proven tools to connect and draw students into the classroom experience. Students need to feel that their own culture is more than OK, it is valid and acceptable to talk about at school. They want to know if the school and staff care enough about them to give them a voice and help foster their vision. Only then are you likely to get students to engage fully.

Help students discover and engage their voice, vision, culture, and history. While voice and vision are powerful, they impact students more at the upper-elementary and secondary levels (5–12) than at the primary level (K–4). But on the other hand, a culturally responsive class at any level (K–12) is a positive step forward in helping your students graduate job or career ready. This empowerment is critical to the formation of a rich classroom climate. Students need teachers that will invest in them socially, emotionally, and cognitively. Without your investment, students feel like they can't invest in school. Don't wait for them. You have to go first.

CHAPTER 16

SET SAFE CLASSROOM NORMS

A key part of the rich classroom climate mindset is the creation of a positive, responsive environment built into a great learning and social environment every day. When students first walk into a classroom, an overarching gestalt of sounds, lighting, people, and room setup tells them whether the environment is a safe, organized, and pleasant place to learn. If a classroom feels safe, students know that only good things will happen to them while they are attending. If the classroom feels safe, students will drop their guard, become less oppositional, and take learning risks. When students do not feel safe or feel unsure about the environment, all bets are off. Your class won't work well because students feel on guard all the time.

Both the teacher and students want a classroom that is clean, interesting, safe, and organized. Students spend over nine hundred hours a year in a classroom. That's nearly a second address for most students and a primary one for those who are homeless, evicted, or in the foster-care system. Together, you can ensure a safe and positive climate.

Physical Safety

To ensure students feel safe, review all safety plans monthly, but focus on the high-probability concerns for that month. At the start of the year, ensure you share safety concerns and procedures for all months, including fire, snow, tornado, floods, or hurricanes. Teach about every chemical, cleaner, or glass product and the safety issues that go with it. Use a hall pass and bathroom pass policy with a simple logbook. Know which students exit and return to your classroom. Avoid sending two

125

students to the restroom in sequence; ensure one has returned before another leaves. In a safe classroom, you have removed obstacles and unsafe objects and set up the groups so that there is easy in-and-out access in case of an emergency. Take a moment before the first day of school and visualize what you would do if there were any of the five most common emergencies (fire, shooting, flooding, storm, or bodily injury). If you can visualize those activities with a smooth transit and safe exit for all your students, you may have a safe classroom.

Emotional Safety

Allowing students to express themselves in a safe environment creates emotional safety. Ensure that students' voices are respected. That means no laughing, smirking, giggling, or degrading opinions. Your standing rule in the classroom to be nice means valuing everyone's opinion. When you see others following this rule, acknowledge it: "Jared, I love the way you jumped in to help your neighbor. That helps our whole class see how being nice works." Consider the following classroom norms.

- When students express their opinions about the news, the neighborhood, or a personal event, always thank them.

- Keep eye contact while a student is speaking. Only break eye contact when you move to another student and have already thanked the contributor.

- Never argue, disregard, or move on to the next student until you thank the student who is speaking ("I appreciate your jumping in" or "Always good to hear from you; hope you jump back in again soon").

- When others interrupt, laugh, make fun of, deride, giggle, or make fun of another student's response, stop the class. Remind students of the class rules and the need for respect and safety. Don't be heavy about this; many students do this with their peers or at home, and it seems normal. Let students know there are two sets of rules; what is inappropriate for class, and what works at home. But still, focus on the good they do. They are a fraction of your age and sometimes show up unprepared for hard work.

Everything you do communicates to your students something about you, them, and the class climate. For most teachers, when students make mistakes, they think it's bad, and the goal is to correct the mistake, push it under the rug, and move on. Bad idea! Think about this for a second; if you want students to be more willing to make mistakes to learn and grow, you'll need to *show* that as a class norm.

Read the following statements, and consider what they all have in common.

- "Check out these options. Now, which one may be your favorite of these answers and why?"
- "I'm glad that you showed me your mistake. That will help me do a better job in teaching you this year."
- If students point out your mistake, you say, "Wow! Thanks for showing me my best mistake this month! Props to you."
- "The reason your wrong answers are helpful is because they tell us in what direction our thinking was off. Now we can correct it and get smarter."
- "I'm going to ask for some answers, but I predict there will be some very different answers, and that's OK. Let's find out if I'm right."

Every one of these responses shows that mistakes are acceptable to make. In class, stop focusing on the answer only. What you really want to know is how the student came up with that answer and his or her assumptions, prior knowledge, and process to get to the answer. This means, when you review or go over a test with the class, ask students to help you understand their path: "Jason, can you jump in and walk us through number four?"

If you routinely expect or anticipate that students will be (or should be) "right," you'll get frustrated and disappointed often. Expect students to make mistakes. The human brain has thrived by being primarily a gist processer. If we get the gist of things, we can survive. However, schools want the exact details, not the gist. Accepting mistakes as opportunities to grow is a new skill that takes time, coaching, and support. The joy in your work is when you can help students walk through the thinking steps, just one at a time, to help them get better answers next time.

Additionally, jump from *good* to *extraordinary* in your feedback. Use positive words in the classroom and be genuine with them. Show passion, and use passionate words. For example:

- "That was *excellent*, nearly *incomparable*!"
- "Hey you were *ridiculously good*!"
- "Now that was, I must say, *sensational* and *sizzling*!"
- "I'm going to call that *exceptional* and *pretty amazing* if I do say so myself!"

Notice the excited, positive language. It puts students *on cloud nine*. It's nearly *breathtaking*. Some might call it *brilliant*, and others might use words like *extraordinary*, *fantastic*, and *tremendous*. Although we just might settle on words like *impressive, magnificent, zestful, unbelievable, remarkable, astonishing, awesome*, and *spot-on*. Say to a student who just surprised you with a great answer, "Now that was *magnificent*! You were *astonishing*!" These words infuse a positive energy, especially when you bolster them with energized body language.

As your demeanor grows from neutral to mildly positive to fully positive, the positivity equips students with the adaptive bias to approach and explore new learning, people, or situations. You need lots of classroom positivity because the effects of negativity that some students get at home are stronger than equal effects of good (Baumeister, Bratslavsky, Finkenauer, & Vohs, 2001). To overcome any classroom toxicity of negatives, apathy, and skepticism, you'll need to not only be a neutral force but also a strong positive force in students' lives (Catalino & Fredrickson, 2011).

Cool Rules

Teachers understand the value of rules. However, one issue I find with them is that when there are too many rules, the harder it is for students to recall and implement them. (The U.S. tax code is over seventy thousand pages long. Is there really any more honest compliance because it is fifty times longer than *War and Peace*? Not likely.)

So do you really need a dozen (or more) classroom rules? To create a climate that works, it is critical that you have very few, but well-understood and well-followed, rules. We call those *cool rules*. Here are four examples.

1. Be nice (be good, fair, and supportive of others).
2. Work hard (come to class prepared to use every minute).
3. Make no excuses (don't blame others or play the victim; be responsible).
4. Choose well (life is full of choices—be thoughtful).

Be Nice

Be nice is a simple but clear rule that everyone can learn to follow. It means no name-calling, hitting, pushing, insulting, poking, teasing, swatting, or criticizing other students or the teacher. To be nice also means saying, "Please," "Thank you," "I'm sorry," and "I was wrong." This rule means no lying, cursing, arguing, tattling, cheating, or cutting in line, as those are not nice. It also means no stealing anything (pencils, pens, laptops, smartphones, watches, jewelry, tablets, iPods, lunches, and so on). After all, taking others' things is not nice. *Be nice* also means students follow directions and raise their hand instead of blurting things out.

Empathy is critical with this rule. You will have to show students how much you believe in it. The teachers who succeed with their students are always the ones who can understand where students are coming from and what their needs are. This means never, ever embarrass or humiliate a student in class. Some students have home lives that are hard to imagine. Don't assume that they are unmotivated (they may be in a temporary funk). Never assume that they don't care (they often have a home emergency like abuse or a death on their mind) or they didn't try to get to class on time (it's possible they're dealing with problems at home or bullies in the streets or the hallway).

When I was six to fifteen, my violent, alcoholic stepmother made my home life a living hell. When I came to class, I was often thinking about what would happen when I went home. I was not unmotivated; I just wanted a teacher who cared enough and made it safe enough for me to forget my problems at home. When you show you care, students feel safer and let their guard down. Then, they can relax and get into the class. That makes for a big win for both the student and for the teacher.

However, if a student says something inappropriate, simply say, "In our class, we don't use those words. Hang on for just a second after class, please." Then, talk to him or her in private after class. Consider the following techniques.

- **Rebuild the relationship:** "Listen, you're a good kid, and I like having you in my class." (Students need to be able to trust you. Your goal is that students feel connected, so they can learn to solve their own problems and work as part of a great team.)

- **Establish relevance:** "I asked you to stay after class, because I really want you to graduate. Remember that job you told me you wanted? You have got to have a degree for it. When you said what you said earlier in class, I got worried. Remember, our first rule is to be nice." (Reduce the meetings about penalties, misbehaviors, and reprimands. Staying after class is not for a punishment. Instead, reserve these private meetings so you can help each succeed. The student may just be bored or frustrated.)

- **Create an ally:** "I'm on your side, and I know you're a good kid, but more importantly, other adults might not know you well. If they heard you say that, they'll go ballistic and maybe try to get you expelled. That might keep you from graduating." (Seek first to understand students. Every word you speak, every move you make, and every thought you hold is either helping or hurting your students' chances of graduating.)

- **Provide a solution:** "What can you do next time, when you're really ticked off, that won't get you in trouble?" (Let students answer, and then ask if they'd like a suggestion.)

- **Reaffirm:** "Here's what I was looking for (*show the student*). Can you do this? Now, just to make sure I said things right, tell me what you heard." (*Let the student review what you talked about.*)

- **Exit the meeting:** "That sounds good. You're on the right track now. Hey, thanks for your time. We'll see you tomorrow. Have a good one."

To foster better behaviors, keep your classroom energy positive. Grumpy, angry students are less susceptible to change than happy students. When students feel happy, their brains release higher levels of dopamine, the neurotransmitter responsible for pleasure, the anticipation of pleasure, working memory, and effort. Higher levels of dopamine are associated with greater synaptic plasticity—the brain's learning process. In short, dopamine is a vital player in the change process in the prefrontal cortex (Sheynikhovich, Otani, & Arleo, 2013). When you add positive reinforcement, the brain changes even faster (Blake, Heiser, Caywood, & Merzenich, 2006). When the classroom climate is positive, change is more likely to happen. Consider the following old and new ways to use positive attitudes in the classroom.

- **Old:** "Class, half of you are looking out the window; pay attention to this."
  New: "Class, I am loving the eyes upfront. This will be awesome, so let's get all eyes on target in the next ten seconds so we can finish on time."

- **Old:** "I only see a few hands up in the air. Let's get those hands up!"
  New: "Class, I am seeing five, eight, and now ten hands up. This is good. Just a few more; now we have fifteen hands—it's almost the whole class!"

- **Old:** "Serena, please wait to answer until Tim decides he can join us."
  New: "Hey, before we get going, some forgot to track upfront so we can go on to the next thing. Give your neighbor a heads-up that our eyeball trackers can help us start."

- **Old:** "You've got the idea, but I want it to be more complex. Can you restate that?"
  New: "Love your idea. Now, let's upgrade to next year's learning and use our two new vocabulary words *ingratiate* and *inordinate* in your answer. Can you do that please? I'll check back with you in one minute."

Being nice is more than a platitude. The science is strong behind this: when students feel good in your class, making good things happen gets easier (Bhullar, Schutte, & Malouff, 2013; Heller et al., 2013). They learn better, feel differently, and behave much better. Create, expect, and reinforce. Do students know the classroom expectations? Do they feel comfortable using them or merely compliant? Use these suggestions for creating a more positive classroom climate.

- Remember to smile when you greet students.
- Never, ever raise your voice to yell, criticize, or complain.
- Create teams that demonstrate team cheers and celebrations.
- Smile when you call on students, make eye contact, and thank them for their effort and risk.
- If your students want to become leaders, encourage them.
- Celebrate the little successes upfront yourself (model the joy).
- Allow students time in each class to get up and move just for fun.
- Never instill fear, make dire predictions, or discourage students.

The beauty of the *Be nice* rule is that it can be applied to nearly every circumstance. It shouldn't necessarily be your only rule. Although for some it is their only rule. Think it through and make a decision.

Work Hard

Work hard is a simple but clear reminder that most good things require preparation, effort, and grit. To work hard means students come to school prepared with their supplies and expect to hit barriers and obstacles. It means switching tactics when you do hit roadblocks. Students may have to ask more questions in class, draw out their problems, ask a peer for help, work with a study buddy, or review their learning to look for clues. If someone else learns faster, the student needs to know he or she is not stupid.

Your framing of effort is critical. Make it clear the real goal of effortful hard work: "The harder you try, the more you succeed" and "Working harder means you can do anything." When you introduce new learning tasks to your students, share the challenges as fun and cool. Always, dismiss the easy tasks as a bit boring and not very useful for the brain. Finally, dismiss the implications that our brains get tired easily. We do not run out of effort as quickly as most think we do (Job et al., 2015). Learning is supposed to be work; if it's not, they're not learning anything new.

Make No Excuses

The easy way out of every problem is to point fingers (lay blame to others) or play lame ("I'm a victim; it wasn't my fault"). But this path fails to promote personal responsibility. This rule is a way to teach students personal responsibility.

No excuses means that when you don't do what you said you would, don't make excuses. State the truth ("I didn't get it done"), and then, if appropriate, apologize ("I am sorry I broke my promise to you"), and finally, fix the problem ("Can I get that to you on Friday?"). This can be a potentially harsh message for students to hear. There's only one way for them to get this message from you: with love.

Again, your empathy is critical. Unless the teacher genuinely cares and looks out for every student, students will tune out. To pull this third rule off in your classroom, you'll need to model it in your own life. When you are tempted to complain, blame others, or play the victim, stop yourself. Remind yourself that your students need a strong role model. You don't need to be perfect; just remember to model this attribute and keep improving on it yourself.

Choose Well

This rule reminds students of the value of self-regulation and the power of choice. We are not responsible for everything that happens to us (such as a drunk driver who almost runs us off the road, a parent passing away, a hurricane or flood, a friend dying, or the loss of a job because of budget cuts), but we are responsible for how we respond.

Your references to having autonomy and choice are critical. Use the word *choice* in positive ways so students see it as a benefit: "You will get to choose the topic on this assignment" and "You made a good choice." If students see choosing as a heavy adult responsibility, they may back off of it. The fact is when students see more sense of autonomy in choice, they will engage more in the classroom (Hafen et al., 2012). We respond to our feelings by making choices. We respond to circumstances by making choices. We respond to pressure, deadlines, and emergencies with choices. The choices you make will reinforce your narrative or create a new one. Teach students that they always have a choice in life. *Choose well* is a reminder of that gift.

Quick Consolidation

Creating an upbeat, emotionally positive class climate is no Pollyanna idea. The science is rock solid. This chapter reminds you to create and maintain norms in your classroom that foster a rich classroom climate. At the beginning, the core reminder is emotional safety. Students have to feel like you will protect them from the risk of bullying. They have to feel that the teacher will not embarrass or humiliate them in front of their peers. If you do those things, you will diminish their emotional safety. Students' predictable response is to reduce engagement and shut down. You can orchestrate the warm, uplifting climate, and students can flourish and bloom. In the next chapter, you'll learn how to foster the academic optimism that boosts achievement.

CHAPTER 17

FOSTER ACADEMIC OPTIMISM

It is likely you've started to see how all of the ideas and strategies in this book work together. For example, if you want to raise expectations, you'll need gutsy goals. However, to make them happen, you'll need more optimism and hope. Plus, you'll have to give better-quality feedback. Every strategy plays off of, and depends on, another strategy. If you're thinking this is quite a complex puzzle, you're right. Welcome to the world of high-performance teaching. Here is the good news: you only need to do one thing at a time. That's it. Do one at a time until it's automatic. Then, you're ready for the next thing. This chapter is all about creating a classroom climate where students *believe* they can achieve crazy high gutsy goals. In school, students understand quickly whether they are good at something (or not). Like most of us, they learn to predict how they'll do in class, based partially on past experiences. This prediction of expectations is important because it regulates how much effort they're willing to expend. As a teacher, you should know why you expend energy to create this type of class climate.

As we've seen previously, the effect size of having an expectation of success is sky-high at 1.44 (Hattie, 2009). That's why from day one highly effective teachers quickly take charge in each new class raising and creating strong new, more optimistic expectations. If you fail to raise the mental and academic bar (with enthusiasm and gutsy goals), you'll allow students to expect and live out low expectations, and that action changes your climate (for the worse). Let's break down academic optimism.

The Climate of Academic Optimism

Years ago, the groundbreaking research on teacher expectations showed what a difference having high academic expectations makes on student achievement (Rosenthal & Jacobson, 1992). Now, the research is narrowing to students of poverty.

Author Yvette Jackson (2011) calls for developing a class climate with a *pedagogy of confidence*, which is both a fearless expectation and the necessary support for high intellectual performance. Jackson's (2011) work shows that students need educators who instill the beliefs of possibility, erase the fears that limit students, and overcome the additional cultural learning barriers students of color face. Jackson is fearless in promoting high levels of cognitive achievement with relationships, respect, and empathy. When you do that in your classroom, academic results will rise.

The common barriers for the poor include biases in labeling, debilitating classroom limitations, and conflicts with cultural differences. In fact, self-affirmation among the poor (but not middle or upper class) can improve the cognitive performance and decision making (Hall, Zhao, & Shafir, 2014). In education, we often get desensitized to the process of labeling students. However, labeling students as a *minority* or being a *low* (bottom 25 percent in classroom scores) student is pejorative and detrimental to student achievement. In fact, not labeling students ranks an impressive 0.61 effect size (top 20 out of 138 factors) in contributing to student achievement (Hattie, 2009). High-performing teachers would never label students as *low*.

Jackson's insightful writing gives educators a powerful path for working with African American students, because the relationship between cognitive success and positive affect is a strong 0.54 effect size (Lyubomirsky, King, & Diener, 2005). The pedagogy of confidence means the teacher believes highly in every student and shows the caring and respect that every student deserves.

Wayne Hoy's work on academic optimism evolved from the field of positive psychology, which shows how we can optimize student well-being to raise student achievement (Hoy, Tarter, & Hoy, 2006). Hoy et al.'s (2006) work defines this goal as, "A school with high academic optimism is a collectivity in which the faculty believes that it can make a difference, that students can learn, and academic performance can be achieved" (p. 145). Use the power of your staff to trust in parents and students to ensure the positive affective response you need.

In chapter 9, you read about Jamie's mathematics class, where he used a football theme to build sky-high optimism and can-do success. Optimism is the theme that unites efficacy, trust, and academic challenge because the synergy of these elements can make the extraordinary become possible. Additionally, leadership can use these themes to change school culture (McGuigan & Hoy, 2006). Finally, this push for an academically positive classroom has a robust 0.67 effect size, placing it well within the upper levels of contributors to student achievement (Hattie, 2009). Now, let's learn five ways this is done in real classrooms: (1) change the roles, (2) show the evidence, (3) change the game, (4) make mastery the endgame, and (5) create a sense of ownership.

Change the Roles

Many teachers have found that the quickest way for students to think differently is to step into another role. In a high-poverty school in New Orleans, English teacher Whitney Henderson (2012) got her students hooked in with a different tool: vision. To shift the student perspective, she asks students to write about two questions. First, they must answer, "Who do you want to be in life?" The *who* is a career label such as teacher, writer, or scientist. The change in student identity is critical. It invites students to begin to get inside the head of that occupation and prompts them to imagine and take on the character traits to be the dream occupation they want to be.

Second, they must answer, "How would a scientist answer this question?" These students are beginning the process of developing their psychological profile and new life narrative for thinking differently, as a successful role model. For example, a scientist would be curious and relentless in the search for answers, and those are the traits the student will take on. This changing of roles can be a powerful shift in mindsets that fosters academic optimism.

Show the Evidence

Katie Lyons, our history teacher from Chicago (see chapter 15), wants her students to know that success is possible, and success can happen in her class. To do this, she records and plays student-produced documentaries and performances (Lyons, 2012). She displays exhibits that former students developed, navigates student-created websites, and shows papers that students have authored. She shows every class what students their own age can do when they reach for the stars. When it is time to ask students to do their best, every student knows this means to shoot for the stars. They can see real, detailed, and concrete examples of what quality work looks like. This kind of evidence gives students the vision and confidence that their goal is doable.

Change the Game

Sometimes students feel that they cannot succeed at a certain task. When you have a sense students feel this way, change the game to improve classroom climate. That means change who the students think they are, what they think about the subject, or who they believe the teacher is.

Every teacher has to sell students on the fact that what they are being asked to do in school is important, relevant, and urgent. As an English teacher, Whitney Henderson (2002) showed books that have altered the course of humanity through powerful writing, telling her students they write to change the world. The books include *The Invisible Man*

(Ralph Ellison) and *Diary of a Young Girl* (Anne Frank). That single message speaks of gutsy goals and a sense of optimism. Students' writing can tell a powerful story about themselves and maybe change the world. By using the Author's Chair activity, where students sit in front of the class in an "author's chair" and read their story, students form a comfort level among peers. Other students may also ask a question or share comments. They are becoming writers who are already changing the world, starting with themselves. The game was changed.

Make Mastery the Endgame

Mastery is a process and destination. For instance, an effective teacher says, "I don't just want them to get it right. I want them to become so proficient that they rarely get it wrong. Only then, we'll move on." The mastery process is about developing a lifelong skill, such as perseverance, that makes complex, challenging learning worthwhile. This factor is not just good teaching. In mastery, there is no trying hard, doing your personal best, or being just good enough. The mastery process is a personal quest. One researcher put mastery at the very top of all strategies for science (Willett et al., 1983). Other researchers find that mastery has a strong effect size of 0.96 on disadvantaged and lower-ability students (Kulik & Kulik, 1987). Hattie (2009) ranks mastery learning as 29 out of 138 factors (top 25 percent) that contribute to student achievement. Mastery can take an extra 10 to 25 percent more classroom time, which is often at a premium. However, the extra time can pay off in improved student performance, which is a big part of the school experience.

To do this, set gutsy goals, as discussed earlier, and continually reinforce the big goal as well as the success made on the micro goals. Share examples of prior students reaching mastery, and point out who is on track to reach mastery. And, remember to celebrate small milestones (micro goals).

Create a Sense of Ownership

Remember to use the words *we* and *us* to say "We're all in this together." This invites students to see the classroom experience as shared. That sharing invites them to be more likely to assert their sense of control over the classroom world (in a good way). They may embrace the opportunity of classroom responsibilities. When students own the climate, everything changes. Ownership comes in many forms.

For example, some schools have embraced discipline programs in which discipline becomes restorative instead of punitive. The premise of this practice is that it is inclusive, collaborative, and rooted in our very early years (Riedl, Jensen, Call, & Tomasello, 2015). There are variations in restorative justice programs, but the essence of the program is about repairing relationships. If a student misbehaves, he or she is given the chance to come forward and make things right. In some cases, he or she sits down in a circle and talks out what happened with the teacher and the other parties. The mediator asks restorative questions like, "What happened? How did it happen? What can we do to make it right?" Ultimately, it all leads to making a plan that all parties can live with, and the relationships are repaired and strengthened. Bottom line, the students are not disciplined.

At the grades K–5 level, you may use cooperative learning and class jobs to empower students. Remember, all K–5 jobs should have recognizable titles that pay real money in the real world. At the grades 6–12 level, you could also have a classroom drawing, list jobs upfront, and have students complete resumes or interviews to fill all the jobs available. These jobs would be for four to six weeks each. Students are welcome to trade jobs with another student if both parties agree. The key feature of ownership is that the job is necessary (and relevant) to help make the class work. Table 17.1 lists jobs for elementary students, with old and new classroom job titles. Table 17.2 (page 138) lists more advanced jobs and descriptions for grades 6–12 students. You could, of course, come up with another dozen much-needed classroom jobs (using the real-world job titles is critical).

Table 17.1: Class Jobs for Grades K–5 Students

Old Title	New Title
Line leader	Tour guide
Caboose	Security officer
Paper passer-outer	Materials handler
Pet monitor	Zookeeper
Bathroom monitor	Bouncer
Teacher helper	Assistant teacher
Plant waterer	Botanist
Fish helper	Marine biologist
Messenger	FedEx or UPS worker
Lights	Electrician

Table 17.2: Class Jobs for Grades 6–12 Students

Title	Description
Chief learning officer (CLO)	The CLO ensures that no one snickers, laughs, makes fun of, or criticizes students in class. The CLO raises his or her hand and says "rerun" whenever there is an infraction, and the offending student apologizes and the student reoffers his or her contribution.
Chief safety officer (CSO)	The CSO says "rerun" for any instances of horseplay, grabbing, trash talking, or unsafe behavior. The offending student will back up and retrace his or her actions, apologizing, if necessary.
IT specialist (ITS) or media specialist	The ITS or media specialist helps keep class technology running smoothly and supports other students (or the teacher) in effectively using it.
Key grip (KG)	The KG acts as a general-purpose handyperson, responsible for setup, lighting, staging, and management.
Communications and publicity specialist (CAPS)	The CAPS shares news, weather reports, class progress on a project, team scores on a recent quiz, or class announcements.
Disk jockey (DJ)	The DJ is responsible for playing teacher-approved music at opportune times (such as when transitioning activities or entering and exiting the class), using the class iPod, computer, or radio. (Consider the following songs: "On Top of the World," Imagine Dragons; "Best Day of My Life," American Authors; "Glad All Over," Carl Perkins; "Positive Vibration," Bob Marley; "Happy," Pharrell Williams; "Enjoy Yourself," The Jacksons.)
Environmental protection agent (EPA)	The EPA ensures that the physical environment is optimized—no trash or debris on the floor, waste gets recycled if possible, and the classroom is clean.

Quick Consolidation

In this chapter, we finally bring to a close the section on creating a rich classroom climate. The chapter began with introducing the research, which shows strong effect sizes for a rich classroom climate. Next, you were introduced to five climate builders. They included changing roles, which allows the students to behave differently, without loss of face. The second tool was showing students clear evidence of the high standards you expect of them. When students see peer work, it can be very inspirational. Third, you might also consider changing the game by reframing the assignment or activity. Fourth, make it less about getting a grade and more about doing something spectacular, like changing the world. The final tool was creating ownership. Without this, the class is always a teacher-run event. Students must have a stake in the game and reason to participate. Give them a sense of control over their daily experiences. It has to become "our class" and be an optimistic one.

CHAPTER 18

LOCK IN THE RICH CLASSROOM CLIMATE MINDSET

The core understanding for a rich classroom climate is that climate matters a great deal, and you influence how your students turn out more than you think you do. Most teachers engage at least one of the strategies introduced in this part, but few engage most or all of them. This part helped peel back the veil behind the high-performing classroom teachers who routinely make two years of academic gains or more for every year they teach. I am inviting you to take up one or two strategies and discover just how powerful the changes can be.

Change the Narrative, Change Your Teaching

Here's a new narrative: the context (academic, emotional, and cultural climate) in which students learn is everything. You are the designer, engineer, and contractor that builds a classroom climate. When you create a great climate for learning, you will foster greatness in students. Now, let's focus on your class climate. What would your narrative say about it? If your narrative is not hopeful, enthusiastic, and optimistic, your class climate may be hurting your students' academic performance. Notice how strong teachers change the narrative (their story), both in their students' lives and their own. Remember, you choose not what happens to you, but you choose how you respond to what happens to you.

I invite you to choose the narrative of yourself not as a victim of your poor climate (lighting, temperature, class size, noise, students, or so on) but as the weather-maker and climate-builder in class. This year could be all about the story of how you create such a rich instructional climate where every student learns and loves to learn. This mindset decision that you are about to make is critical; you are saying, "I focus on what students need to succeed and build it into the learning and social environment every day." See figure 18.1.

You Are Your Mindset: Which Is Yours?

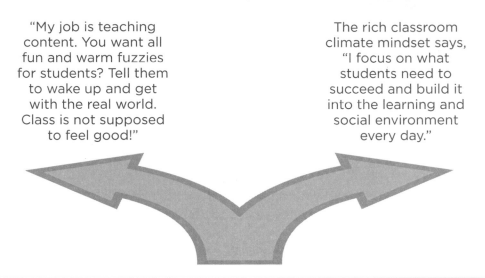

"My job is teaching content. You want all fun and warm fuzzies for students? Tell them to wake up and get with the real world. Class is not supposed to feel good!"

The rich classroom climate mindset says, "I focus on what students need to succeed and build it into the learning and social environment every day."

Figure 18.1: You are your mindset—the rich classroom climate mindset.

Fill in the following blanks with your name and a strategy from this mindset. Repeat the phrase daily until it's automatic.

"I, _____, am committing to developing the rich classroom climate mindset in my students every single day. I will begin with one of the strategies mentioned, which is _____. I will continue this until I have mastery and it's automatic. At that point, I'll learn something new to foster student success."

Reflection and Decision

Create the optimal conditions for learning; put people first, and everything else second. The first time I visited another teacher's class that had an amazing instructional climate, I saw her start with one quick strategy (a "turn to your neighbor" affirmation). Then, she added another (an energizer) and other activities (she smiled when calling on every student and thanked each one). The effect was subtle at first; I could tell something was going on, but there was no immediate ah-ha. Instead, what I saw, heard, and felt was a carefully orchestrated classroom in which it was simply a great place to learn.

Within about twenty minutes, the classroom was active, positive, and safe. There was a sense of community working toward a common (and gutsy) goal. The students and the teacher co-created a great place to learn. The key is to create a classroom environment where students become their best. Does your classroom foster greatness? If not, reread these strategies to find the tool you need to move forward.

Quick Consolidation

This mindset has focused on the rich classroom climate. Over the last few chapters, you have seen multiple ways you can foster a great classroom climate. First, you saw how much relevance matters. Without it, students lose interest. You also saw the power of voice and vision. That is the process of students seeing themselves in the learning. Then, we added the fundamental basics of physical and emotional safety. Use fewer, not more, rules. In the last chapter, you saw the power of academic optimism. That included having high expectations, ownership, and roles and even changing the game. Is every idea here brand new? No, but as I say often, never confuse familiarity with engagement.

The fact is, the number-one influencer over the classroom climate is the teacher. You might say, "No, my students create the climate!" Actually, if you are not proactive, you are right. The climate will emerge, on its own, by the students, if you do nothing. This is a reminder, take the opportunity and seize it!

PART FOUR

WHY THE ENGAGEMENT MINDSET?

CHAPTER 19

SECRETS OF THE ENGAGEMENT MINDSET

Engagement means different things to different people, especially those in academia. For example, you can find constant references to why engagement should be cognitive engagement. However, useful engagement happens on many levels. For example, just keeping your students in quality, alert emotional states is important. In the next few chapters, you will be introduced to several levels of engagement and strategies to use immediately. Teachers who use high engagement and engage with relentless affirming interactions and thoughtful error correction usually have high-performing students (Valentine & Collins, 2011).

The Engagement Mindset

We have all seen and experienced a classroom where the teacher struggles with purposeful engagement. Predictably, the teacher in that class has a different thought process than that of a highly engaging teacher. The following teacher comments might characterize a struggling teacher's mindset.

- "The students just sit there and sleep. What am I supposed to do if they didn't get enough sleep at home?"

- "We have a ton of content to cover, and sometimes lecture is the best way to do it quickly."

- "I spend half my time disciplining the students. All they do is talk. Anything engaging causes students to be all over the place. I can't take the risks."

- "The engagement strategies I've seen are all a bunch of fluff. How do I know they do any good?"

You'll notice that, at the core of all of these statements, is a sense of powerlessness. There is a sense that engagement is either not possible, a waste, or just too risky. The greater your skill level, the greater your confidence level. Teaching should feel like a powerful job, not a hopeless one.

As a former teacher and staff developer, I can live with teaching that is out of the box, old school, or a bit rigid, but I cannot stomach boredom in students or powerlessness in staff. I cannot accept, mentally or emotionally, students sitting listless and disconnected. Students don't need teachers who accept this version of instruction. Using video clips of a lecture and hiring a student aid to monitor the class would be just as effective.

Engagement is that important. As crazy as it sounds, learning should tickle students' curiosity, inspire them with role models and heroes, grab them by the scruff of the neck, and serenade them through the highs and lows of emotions to something meaningful. Learning is something that students should feel, make, build, talk about, collaborate with others on, and write about. Learning is something that students need to debate, reflect on, and take positions on. Learning has to engage students in ways that make it worth doing. When you're not engaging students, achievement drops (Valentine, 2005). The engagement mindset says, "I can and will engage with purpose every student, every day, every nine minutes or less, guaranteed."

> The engagement mindset says, "I can and will engage with purpose every student, every day, every nine minutes or less, guaranteed."

By contrast, teachers who have highly engaging classes think about their work differently. These teachers (and hopefully you too) see engagement at the heart and soul of learning. All learning should be engaging. The following teacher comments might characterize an engagement mindset.

- "I would never go back to the way it was before. Almost everything we do is engaging. It's way more fun for me and the students."
- "My students love staying engaged. They stay more focused and on task."
- "I don't know any other way to teach. The students look forward to class every day. There's always something we can do to keep them active and contributing."

- "I just learned to add one thing at a time. Over the years, my classes just got more engaging and now my students really like my classes."

The engagement mindset is powerful. There are no excuses, qualifiers, or "as long as the students are good" (or "do their part") variables to the equation. If you don't yet have a highly engaging class, keep reading.

A Hard Look at the Evidence

Secondary students spend over a quarter of their day in disconnected learning states, such as boredom (Shernoff, Csikszentmihalyi, Schneider, & Shernoff, 2003). The majority of secondary students report that they are bored in every single class (Yazzie-Mintz, 2007a). Even upper-elementary students spend the majority of their time (91 percent) sitting solo, without activities or socialization (Pianta, Belsky, Houts, & Morrison, 2007). Yet, continuous classroom engagement consistently ranks high as a contributor to student achievement (Marks, 2000). In fact, a lack of classroom engagement has been cited as the top reason for student dropouts (Rumberger, 2004). Can you help prevent this?

Ongoing classroom engagement fosters learning, with robust contributions to achievement (Appleton, Christenson, & Furlong, 2008; Ladd & Dinella, 2009). Engagement may involve high-cognitive processing, but it is also critical for keeping learners in positive emotional states and for learners having positive school experiences (Reyes et al., 2012). Learning influences and even orchestrates optimal mind and body states.

Our states are minute-by-minute mind and body experiences. We experience anxiety, hope, fear, anticipation, comfort, curiosity, and a host of other states. While they fluctuate all day, we all have a baseline (Raichle et al., 2001), but it's not a motivating baseline state for most students. The more quality minutes per day of learning, the more productive class time is for students and the higher the achievement. Teachers are less likely to get high test scores when students are either disruptive or apathetic, and students are in those states quite often (Eldridge, Galea, McCoy, Wolfe, & Graham, 2003).

In a healthy, high-performing classroom, you'll commonly have states of hope, confidence, reflection, curiosity, confusion, expectancy, camaraderie, and celebration. In low-performing classrooms, you'll often see states of apathy, disconnect, anger, frustration, and maybe even fear. Figure 19.1 (page 150) simplifies classroom states into a select few. This way you can see the states you want in your class (those that are bold) and the opposing state on the opposite side. Make it your mission to cultivate the positive states that lead to positive behaviors and better scores.

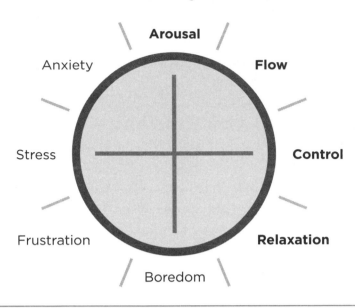

Figure 19.1: Student states.

A baseline state in our brain is fundamental to the understanding of our students' brains. Defining a baseline state in the human brain, arguably our most complex system, poses a difficult challenge. Yet findings confirm the presence of a *default network* in the brain—the activation state present when the brain is not engaged in any specific cognitive task (Raichle et al., 2001). The baseline default mode of brain function is suspended during specific goal-directed behaviors. Then, it goes back to the default network. In short, your students have their own favorite baseline states by default. If their baseline state is a counterproductive one, you'll have to be far more proactive in influencing student states. Otherwise you'll be left wondering, "Why are my students so bored or angry?"

The next few chapters will empower you to make changes in order to engage students. Moving students from bad states to better states is what strong teachers do every day. At first, this process takes extra time and energy. But, over time, and like other skills, it will become automatic. That will give you all of your joy back in teaching.

Quick Consolidation

Why manage your students' states? States (those mind-body moments like joy or apathy) are critical to learning (Immordino-Yang & Damasio, 2007), and most students, from elementary to secondary, are terrible at managing their own states. In the following chapters, you'll read about three strategies for engagement.

1. Engage for maintenance and stress.
2. Engage for setup and buy-in.
3. Engage to build community.

In the next three chapters, we begin digging into engagement. If you're wondering, "How on earth will I get students who are poorly disciplined, apathetic, and angry to make changes?" lean in, and read closely. This engagement process will take some time; it's not a one-day miracle cure. Let's jump into the first type—engagement for maintenance and stress.

CHAPTER 20

ENGAGE FOR MAINTENANCE AND STRESS

Your goal in the classroom is to maintain healthy student states of mind and body. If you don't influence their states, you're at the whim of random states or bad states. Students constantly seek something that will shift and help them manage their states (a text, a party, alcohol, a movie, a boyfriend or girlfriend, food, sports, and so on) because they rarely have strong self-regulation skills. Although engagement can affect other chemicals (cortisol, serotonin, and so on), you'll notice in figure 20.1 (page 154) that simple activity bumps up the heart rate and norepinephrine and dopamine levels. An increased heart rate means greater circulation and oxygen to the brain. Increased norepinephrine in moderate amounts can bump up long-term memory and narrow attentional focus. Boost dopamine, and you get a better working memory, greater effort, and stronger neural plasticity to make changes.

While most teachers want more higher-order engagement, the reality is that while our brain works pretty fast (Buonomano, 2014), students still rarely go from a state of zero activity to high energy in a short amount of time (Halassa et al., 2014). It takes a classroom of constantly managed states to get the quality learning you want. As you know, you won't get higher-order thinking if students are drowsy, bored, and disconnected.

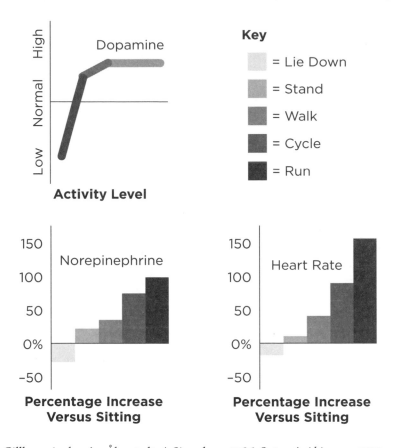

Source: *Gillberg, Anderzén, Åkerstedt, & Sigurdson, 1986; Sutoo & Akiyama, 2003.*

Figure 20.1: Physical activity alters brain chemistry.

Engage to Maintain

Many engagement strategies, which activate arousal states, go by very quickly and maintain mind-body states for optimal learning. Students might not notice many of them. Arousal states are a critical ingredient for paying attention and being receptive to your presence, activities, and content. When teachers activate these arousal states, responsiveness goes up (Hasenstaub, Sachdev, & McCormick, 2007). The truth is, in your class, nothing will work unless students are alert, focused, and in a receptive frame of mind. Without these states, you'll have to reteach content, and students will get bored.

Use basic state-management tools to keep students active, focused, and interacting with you or their peers. These keep students in behaviorally flexible states and promote curiosity, attention, and blood flow. These actions maintain optimal brain chemistry by eliciting the appropriate levels of serotonin (for attention, behavioral flexibility, and comfort), noradrenaline (focus and memory), dopamine (mood, effort, and neural plasticity), and cortisol (for memory and energy).

Many students, particularly the poor, have had adverse home-life experiences, which foster the biological residue of chronic and acute stress (Evans & English, 2002). These students often feel hopeless, depressed, or hypervigilant (Landis et al., 2007). The following seven activities are short and physical to influence the mind and body in the easiest and quickest way possible. Just physical movement alone can enhance blood flow and productive neurochemicals that enhance cognition (Tomporowski, Davis, Miller, & Naglieri, 2008).

You can modify the activities for developmental age and, over time, your students can lead them. Incorporating a simple activity every ten to fifteen minutes (or less) will keep students engaged. Check out the following seven examples. These are all easy, but as a group, they are quite powerful. Each focuses on a simple goal, such as arousal to maintain states of alertness.

1. **Repeat after me:** Students repeat what the teacher says—"Today we focus on two core ideas. How many are we focusing on?" (Class responds: "Two!")

2. **Turn to:** This strategy occurs after a student success—"Turn to your neighbor and say, 'Great effort.'"

3. **Clap-boom-clap:** Students pay attention to listen to each clap and participate—"Follow along with me. I clap once, and you repeat. Every time I double clap, you say 'Boom!' That tells me you're reading for something big! Are you ready?"

4. **Physical acts:** Students are usually eager to move around—"Quick! Let's find a new partner. Slide your chair a foot to the side, and rotate it to find a new neighbor."

5. **Attention-getters:** This strategy especially appeals to students who are bored or have lost focus—"If you're ready for something new, clap twice, and say, 'Yes!'" Or, "If you want to try out an experiment, stomp your feet twice, and please stand up."

6. **Ownership strategies:** Students want to feel ownership over their work—"If you've got your handout, hold it up high, and say, 'I got mine.' Now, put your name on it. Great. Now, look on your neighbor's paper, and if he or she doesn't have a name on it, wake him or her up."

7. **Call and response:** This strategy creates quick refocus routines—"Class up!" (The students respond, "That's us!") Or, "Mind up!" (The students respond, "That's me!")

Without engagement strategies, students may feel lethargic, and it becomes harder to engage them the longer that state sets in. The seven strategies will help teachers maintain student arousal levels. However, if students are experiencing high or low stress, you might use any of the following strategies in the next section.

Engage to Manage Stress

We used to think that genes and environment were separate, isolated factors. The field of epigenetics has taught us that our environments can actually influence (suppress or activate) our genes and influence adolescent behaviors (Keshavan, Giedd, Lau, Lewis, & Paus, 2014). Our thoughts, words, and actions enact consistent and clear changes in the genes (Dusek et al., 2008). This process is called *epigenetic changes*, meaning life experiences act on our genes to either suppress their programming or activate them. Some stress is good and other stress (chronic) is bad for the body and mind. The ideal amount of stress for learning is the top (middle) third of the curve in figure 20.2. Too little stress or too much is counterproductive.

The Yerkes–Dodson Stress Productivity Curve

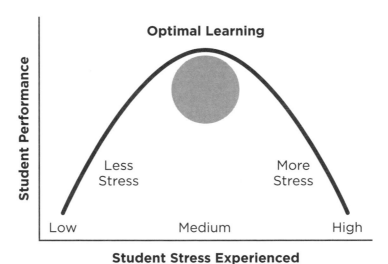

Figure 20.2: Stress productivity curve.

We all generate stress, apathy, or distress through two filters: (1) relevance and (2) sense of control. How do you manage to keep students in this fine-grained optimal zone for stress? The secret is to involve students in the process. Students will adjust the levels of their work to get to the sweet spot. In order to help students manage their own stress, keep the relevance high, and give students some sense of control over the process. This feeling of being in control is critical (Santiago, Etter, Wadsworth, & Raviv, 2012).

When students are not being productive, you can reconnect them to the relevance of the topic or help them raise or lower their stress. Use destressors when students seem too anxious, stressed, or out of control. Raise stress when energy is low. Following are three quick K–12 activities that help students connect and control their stress with the one thing closest to them—their body. First, do these with your class and describe how and why they work. Then, over time, allow students to lead groups or the whole class.

1. **Extend, compact, and release series:** Students stand up and complete a series of movements that either stretch out their limbs (stand on tiptoes and then relax, extend each leg forward and then release, then move a step backward with one leg and then relax, or press palms tightly together and then release). These activities can help with boosting well-being and lowering stress (Carlson, Collins, Nitz, Sturgis, & Rogers, 1990).

2. **Fluid movements:** Students stand with knees slightly bent, and move arms in slow, grand sweeping circular movements, creating swirls or shaping images (as is done with tai chi or hula) with their hands. When done purposefully, they'll reduce stress and gain attention and creativity (Slepian & Ambady, 2012).

3. **Mindful breathing:** Students stand up and practice a series of inhales and exhales on a slow ascending path of deeper breathing. First, they'll inhale through the nose and hold it to the count of two and exhale. This has shown to benefit secondary students (Noggle, Steiner, Minami, & Khalsa, 2012), middle school students (Terjestam, Jouper, & Johansson, 2010), and elementary students (Kim et al., 2002).

Alternatively, how do you raise the good stress with your students? The good stress goes up when we feel a sense of control and excitement at the same time. Here are some of your potential good stress-inducing strategies: physical activity (walk, stomp, act out, dance, or role-play), music (making it or listening to it), cooperation (or competition), deadlines (urgency), and a leader (student, teacher, or soundtrack). The evidence is overwhelming that physical activity supports learning, behavior, and cognition. Physical activity helps develop attentional performance (Budde, Voelcker-Rehage, Pietrabyk-Kendziorra, Ribeiro, & Tidow, 2008), executive functions (Best, 2010), academic achievement (Coe, Pivarnik, Womack, Reeves, & Malina, 2006), and behaviors (Mahar et al., 2006).

Each of the following activities is convenient and has strong results in cognition and behavior management. Several of these, using familiar childhood games, have been found to be a positive contributor (three to four months ahead of peers) to student achievement (Wanless, McClelland, Acock, Chen, & Chen, 2011; Wanless, McClelland, Tominey, & Acock, 2011). Consider the following nine activities.

Simon Says

This common game can improve self-regulation. First, do the typical starter format to show students how to behave. Then, mix up Simon's commands. Say, "Only do the first of the two commands." Then, give two quick back-to-back directions such as, "Simon says, 'Clap your hands.' Simon says, 'Stomp your feet.'" This is perfect for younger students at the K–3 level, and, with modifications, can be very tough for secondary students too.

Walk to the Music

Select five to seven pieces of music. Ensure that they are all very different in pacing, style, and genre. For example, my list includes the following: "Tequila" (the Champs), "Push It" (Salt-N-Pepa), the *Rocky II* soundtrack, "Happy" (Pharrell Williams), and "Java" (Al Hirt). Students stand up and listen for directions. Students' assignment is to move to each song's beat or pacing. Play each song for about fifteen to twenty seconds, and then go to the next one. On the last song, all students head back to their seats. Make up your own song list. As long as you use age-appropriate music this works at every grade level.

Head-to-Toes and Head-Toes-Knees-Shoulders

These familiar activities, in which teachers instruct students to touch their head, toes, knees, or shoulders and also perform an opposite action, are helpful when introducing literacy and mathematics. The Head-to-Toes task (for younger students) and the Head-Toes-Knees-Shoulders task (for older students) require students to integrate attention, working memory, and inhibitory control. In a study of 814 students in four countries (United States, Taiwan, South Korea, and China), these tasks measured behavioral regulation and predicted early academic success on pre and post scores for vocabulary and mathematics (Wanless, McClelland, Acock et al., 2011). This suggests that the activity requires, develops, and uses skills that have an academic payback.

Drumbeats

Use drumbeats to trigger different actions that students do while sitting (like clapping or stomping) or walking. For example, students walk quickly to fast drumming and slowly to slow drumming and freeze when the drumming stops. You may also ask students to respond to opposite cues, such as walking slowly to fast drumbeats or stomping their feet for slow drumming.

Red Light, Green Light

The teacher acts as the stoplight and stands across from students in a line. He or she holds up a red or green stoplight sign alternately to represent stop and go, and students move closer and stop as necessary. Over time, teachers can switch the colors, such as purple for *go* and orange for *stop*. Then, they can alternate the colors. Using different shapes is also effective. For example, a yellow square for *go* and a yellow triangle for *stop*. Students can also take turns being the stoplight.

Orchestra Conductor

In this simple activity, every student uses his or her own musical instrument (real or imagined). The leader uses a drumstick or pencil as a conducting baton. When the conductor waves the baton, students play their instruments at the same rate as the speed of the baton. Then, the teacher can reverse the directions, asking students to move slowly when the baton goes fast. Establish a baseline of expected cues, then reverse them and speed them up.

Touch and Go

In this activity, the teacher plays music and gives students simple, easy tasks. For example, he or she may ask students to circle two tables, touch three walls, touch two objects made of wood, or touch the backs of eleven chairs. Students return to their seats when the music stops. The teacher can also give them a specific amount of time to do the tasks, such as sixty seconds. Activities like these can bump up a student's dopamine levels (for working memory, plasticity, and effort) and noradrenaline (aiding focus and long-term memory), which help learning and attention (Gillberg et al., 1986).

High Ten, Low Ten

For this fun activity to engage students, find some good dance music with a rhythmic backbeat (such as the Pretenders's "Don't Get Me Wrong"). Students each have one partner, facing each other two feet apart. Both raise their hands and hit each other's hands with a high ten, then lower their hands to knee level and hit hands again in a low ten. The fun of this activity is in doing it quickly, until you get a rhythm. Then, add two more partners to form a diamond-shaped group of four. Students keep their original partners across from them but have new partners to the left and right. When one twosome gives each other a high ten, the other twosome gives each other a low ten. Once groups coordinate that rhythm in a foursome, they can add other challenges like spins, crossover claps, or so on.

Old Dance or New Dance

This activity is done in a team. Team members rise, and when the music starts, the leader points to a person standing and says, "Old or new?" The teammate chooses either an existing dance step he or she knows (affirming prior knowledge) or invents a new one. All other teammates follow along for forty-five seconds of pure fun.

Quick Consolidation

In this chapter, we introduced two types of engagement. The first is for maintaining student energy. You can modify any activity that seems too easy or too hard. Remember you are the weather-maker in your classroom. If you sell the activity with enthusiasm and have rapport with students, they'll give it a try. Remember that all learning is state dependent, so if your students are in poor states for learning (such as apathy, boredom, frustration, anger, or distrust), you're wasting their time and yours. The other strategy is to manage stress with destressors (lowering it through fluid movements, deep breathing, and tense and release activities). Too much and too little stress is ineffective for learning. Once you become more purposeful about maintaining healthy student states and managing stress, you'll have more time in your classroom because you'll spend less time reteaching and more time celebrating the learning.

CHAPTER 21

ENGAGE FOR SETUP AND BUY-IN

The effectiveness of activities or content blocks typically depend on how well you prepare learners before you begin instruction. Remember, relevance is everything to students' brains. Chapter 14 (page 109) introduced the power of relevance and the essentialness of using student voice and vision in a culturally responsive classroom. However, you'll still need to often rehook students into engagement.

In short, buy-in is priceless for any learning activity, and without it, even good activities will die. Buy-in practically ensures the next task you do will work and the lesson will be more effective. How? The students will pay close attention and save the learning in their brain. Remember, if the brain's not buying into the content, the brain's not changing. If the brain's not changing, you're wasting your time. Creating behavioral relevance may be the most powerful skill you can master. With it, students will remember what you teach (Adcock, Thangavel, Whitfield-Gabrieli, Knutson, & Gabrieli, 2006; O'Keefe & Linnenbrink-Garcia, 2014). See figure 21.1.

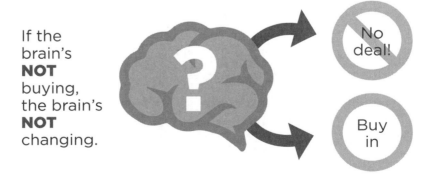

If the brain's **NOT** buying, the brain's **NOT** changing.

No deal!

Buy in

Figure 21.1: Deal or no deal?

Using Setup and Buy-In Strategies

There are two types of classroom learning: (1) compliance ("OK, I guess I can do this") and (2) choice learning ("This sounds good; I will jump in and give it my best"). Over fifty million U.S. students attend school, and many are compliant learners. According to the High School Survey of Student Engagement with over eighty thousand participants, 58 percent of students attend school because it's the law, and 68 percent attend because their friends are there (Yazzie-Mintz, 2007b). That is not a rousing endorsement of our teaching colleagues.

I want more learning to be the "good" type of learning. Compliance learning invites reteaching in your classroom. Why? Motivated, choice learning is more likely to stick (get remembered). Compliance learning means students go through the motions, but they rarely recall learning. Motivating your students before the learning (versus assuming they bought into what you are doing) is critical. Unless the brain perceives the task to be behaviorally relevant, it does not save or remember the learned task (Green & Bavelier, 2008).

A teacher who opens a lesson with a problem to solve, a puzzle, a game, or a joke is likely building up and hoping for student arousal. Those are not bad ideas, they are just not buy-in. Arousal means the student is awake, alert, and in a good metabolic state for potentially learning something. But that is not the same as a state of buy-in, which is a yearning, hungry state that must be fulfilled (Adcock et al., 2006). Buy-in says to the learner, "This is worth learning, pay attention and save it!"

I cannot emphasize this enough: unless you get buy-in from your students every single time you introduce new content, an activity, or anything you want their brain to save, you risk students forgetting it. The human brain is driven by behavioral relevance. It is as if the brain says, "Why should I care about this? Because if I really should care about it, I'll remember it!"

Distinguishing Between Setup and Buy-In

So, let's pause and distinguish between *arousal hooks* (setup) and *buy-in*. Check out the following list.

- Teacher enthusiasm (incites arousal)
- Compelling relevancy (is the holy grail for buy-in)
- Urgency or excitement (invokes arousal hooks)
- Anticipation or curiosity (invokes arousal hooks)
- Novelty (creates curiosity)

- Props or costumes (activate curiosity and arousal)
- Problem solving (invites a state of challenge)

You can see from the list that there are many shades of buy-in. The best one is *compelling relevancy*, but others have some lower-level buy-in—arousal. But arousal is still a good thing to invoke. If your students are sleeping or bored, nothing good is happening for learning. But to get students to learn with energy and momentum, both arousal and buy-in are critical. The following arousal strategies can hook readers into your learning and they are simple and sweet. The idea is to get students to nibble at a good idea until they want to eat up the rest of the learning. These six hooks introduce the content. (Note the bold words as the hooks.)

1. "Now, let's tie in what we just did to what will be on the **test**. First, grab a pencil."

2. "Here's an idea to help you **get the grade you deserve**."

3. "Oh! I've got a great idea; it'll only take a moment. First, stand up please." (The hook is curiosity.)

4. "I'm going to share something that will boggle your mind!" (The hook is anticipation.)

5. "First, take in a deep breath. Now, if you're ready for something **awesome** to learn, stomp your feet twice."

6. "I've got an idea that might **cut your time spent** with your head in a book. It should take just a few minutes. Are you game?"

You could divide your classroom hooks into sections such as kinesthetic (what students can make, toss, play, catch, and act out), props (what you can show or pass around), safari (take your students outside the classroom or go on short field trips), music (set the tone, create an effect, highlight a concept, and use song lyrics), or visual arts (create a poster or lighting change). You could also use theater (become a character or act out an idea or event), hobbies (have a student or you share a hobby, then tie it into the content), or autonomy (allow students to create their own sources for connections). You might use current events (tie in news or pop culture), mystery bag or box (create a special bag or box with a content-relevant item inside), interior design (change the room by altering setup, clearing out chairs, or making it a theme party), and costumes (wear a scarf, hat, or full outfit to portray a character). Table 21.1 (page 164) offers some tips to hook elementary and secondary students.

For any K–12 teacher, there are at least fifty or more hooks you can use. See *Teach Like a Pirate* (Burgess, 2012) for elementary students and *How to Motivate the Reluctant Learner* (R. Jackson, 2011) for specific secondary ideas.

Table 21.1: Elementary and Secondary Social Hooks

Elementary Social Hooks	Secondary Social Hooks
• Next grade level as a challenge or draw • Simple privilege • Fun • Raw teacher enthusiasm • Deep curiosity • Positive affirmation • Grossness • Friendship • Physical activity • Cool mystery	• Edgy and risky activities • Peer pressure • A strong challenge • Stairstepping the activity • Working with friends • Status • Experiments • Finding their voice • Local problems • Working for something huge • College • Competition • New relationships

In previous chapters, you read about Jamie, a secondary mathematics teacher, who uses multiple hooks to pull students into the process and sell them on each strategy. Working with mostly high-poverty secondary students, he uses a key college-entry mathematics score (the one students need to have a chance for a scholarship) as a buy-in for the free-schooling process. He also uses the mathematics score of a nearby school as a competitive ("You are as good as them") buy-in strategy. His use of high-performance teaching tools helps you understand why his results are strong (Irish, 2012).

Asking Questions for Buy-In

Good questions can evoke curiosity, relevance, and reflection. Great questions can change class climate or even student lives. A whole-class question and answer session, when done well, has a strong effect size of 0.81, contributing nearly two years' worth of student achievement (Hattie, 2009), but it is no easy task. It requires participation, inquiry with safety, and a clear goal of deeper understandings while maintaining relationships.

To get started, post the following questions on the board, a screen, or a flipchart. Then, start calling on everyone. If you want to mix up the process a bit, put a jar, basket, or bowl upfront filled with student names, and then call on someone to pick a name (students are immune if they pick their own name). If a student is called on and doesn't know the answer, ask him or her to say, "I don't know, but I'd like to know. Give me a minute, and call on me again." Then, come back to the student a minute later, when he or she is ready. Here are powerful questioning groups you can pull from.

- **Discovery questions:** When students begin a unit or are initially behind, help them find some cognitive footing with discovery questions. Find out their prior knowledge by learning the labels, facts, fragments, and assumptions they have. For example, you might ask, "What do you already know about the Civil Rights Movement in the 1960s?"

- **Essential questions:** These questions elevate the quality and depth of learning by embracing and using relevant interests (McTighe & Wiggins, 2013). There are two types of essential questions: (1) broad (the point goes beyond a unit to a larger, transferable idea such as "What defines a great leader?") and (2) content specific (answerable through a unit's content, such as "After reading *Catch-22*, how do you think you would cope in another world of earlier wars— Yossarian's—and why?").

- **Summarizing-the-content questions:** Students grasp the content and make some statements about it. "What is this about? What is the key understanding? What are two or three key points here? What is a good title for this text? How would you describe the learning in one or two sentences?"

- **Elaborative questions:** Before asking elaborative questions, establish a basic understanding of the content with students. Students should be clear on the talking points and able to summarize the content. Elaborative questions detail unique features or properties of the learning ("What makes tectonic plates so unpredictable?") and potential conflicts ("Why did the Occupy Wall Street group protest? What is its position, and what do the opposing arguments say?").

- **Evidence-gathering questions:** Here, students use reasoning and argumentation to support claims that they make about any statements, arguments, or positions. For example, "Tell me why you feel that your position is a valid one. What makes it any different than the opposition's? What would your opponent say and why? How would you rebut them? What facts support your position that others don't have?"

For those who do contribute, expect more. Ask students, "How do you know that is true (or false)?" When students respond to any answer, say, "Thank you. I appreciate you jumping in. I enjoyed hearing your contributions. Now tell me a bit more." Keep the conversation alive by asking more questions: "How do you know that might be true?"

Remember to do this process with love; respect student concerns for how their peers see and hear them. Never, ever embarrass a student in class. The idea here is simple: discover, probe, and push in a respectful way that appreciates what every student knows and how each can grow.

Quick Consolidation

In this chapter, we introduced two types of engagement: setup (arousal states) and buy-in (behavioral relevancy). Both of these states are critical to the work you do. Arousal states ensure no one is nodding off, losing energy, slumping over, or disconnecting. When you see those behaviors, do something! As noted previously, the best system is to have all your students in either cooperative groups (K–5) or teams (secondary). That way, your class knows that every twenty minutes or so, everyone gets up and moves his or her body by following the stretch trainer or energizer leader.

Buy-in is fundamental to all classroom learning, or students might not learn (or at the least, they won't recall it). You have seen that asking the right questions is one of the best ways to get buy-in. When students buy in, they say, "I want to learn this. It is important to me." Become more purposeful about implementing setup and buy-in, and you'll get more chances to celebrate the learning.

CHAPTER 22

ENGAGE TO BUILD COMMUNITY

The goal of this chapter is to build a classroom community of engaged learners. Building a sense of community fosters academic optimism and reduces inappropriate student behavior. In this chapter, I discuss solving common problems, using reciprocal teaching, and celebrating small whole-class victories.

Solving Common Problems

What are common recurring classroom problems? Examples include starting class on time, having students be quiet, and finishing up on time. To automate a solution to these problems, introduce a special type of community-building activity—a ritual. How is a ritual different from any other classroom activity? Class routines, or rituals, are short preplanned events that help solve recurring problems with positive energy. These activities build camaraderie and promote an inclusive culture. Class rituals have just five criteria to make them work. They must (1) solve a recurring problem, (2) include and engage all students, (3) be simple and easy to do, (4) be predictable, and (5) end on a positive emotional state. Most teachers have procedures that may meet some of these criteria, but rituals meet every single one. They are so simple that it's as if you simply press play to solve a problem when you initiate a ritual. See figure 22.1 (page 168).

Teachers design rituals to engage more of the class socially and build community. How? It is something everyone in the class does together to solve a common problem. You can start one during the first week of class, and then use it semesterlong or yearlong.

What Makes for Highly Effective Classroom Rituals?

1. **They solve a recurring problem**
   (or students won't see the relevancy).

2. **They include and engage everyone**
   (or you'll lose the participation).

3. **They are simple and easy to do**
   (students must be able to automate them).

4. **They are predictable**
   (students should be ready for them every time).

5. **They must end on a positive emotional state**
   (or students won't keep doing them).

Rituals allow you to press play.

Figure 22.1: Highly effective rituals.

Here are some priceless classroom routines that help the whole class solve problems together.

- **Callbacks:** Start class in the morning, after recess, or after a task with a callback—"If you made it to your seat on time, raise your hand and say 'Yes!' Now, turn to your neighbor and say, 'Welcome back!'"

- **End-of-class celebrations:** End the class with a celebration. Students stand and share a learning highlight from the class with another teammate. Then, they put both hands far out to their left and right sides and bring them together with a big clap and say "Yes!"

- **Attention-getters:** Use a whistle and say, "Students, when I have a *really important* idea, I want to know if you're on board. When I blow my train whistle, everyone says 'All aboard!' Now, let's try it out."

Notice these rituals meet the five criteria from figure 22.1. Within three to five weeks, you'll notice that your students may habituate to an activity, a song, or a ritual, and you'll need to change it. The beauty of these is that everyone does them at the exact same moment, on cue, every time. Every student goes into the same state, saying the same words. This is a unity builder, and these are priceless in your classroom. Do not dismiss these because they seem too simple or may not be for older students. I have used them with all K–12 students.

Using Reciprocal Teaching

Reciprocal teaching is a strong complementary factor that can strengthen engagement and, ultimately, student achievement (Rosenshine & Meister, 1994). When done well, it is a very powerful learning tool in the top 20 percent of all classroom strategies (Petty, 2006). Reciprocal teaching involves teaching students specific comprehension-fostering strategies. Students learn four strategies: (1) asking questions about the text, (2) summarizing what was read, (3) predicting what might happen next, and (4) attempting to clarify words and phrases that were not understood. Using reciprocal teaching, the teacher gradually releases responsibility, so the student gets better and better.

Initially, students might read a paragraph, and then the teacher might explicitly model the process of using these strategies on a selected text. Next, the students practice the strategies on the next section of text, and the teacher supports each student's work with coaching, hints, and explanations. The teacher gradually releases responsibility so that the student can teach it to his or her peers. The effect size for reciprocal teaching is a huge 0.74, ranking it high among teacher interventions (Hattie, 2009). That's almost a year and a half of gains. Although, students see teachers teach, they don't understand the processes of quality teaching. To get the value out of reciprocal teaching, you'll need to model it. To build comprehension, consider using the following key strategies after exposing students to the content (Palincsar & Brown, 1984). First, ask students to find a partner. Their partner can be a long-term study buddy or a temporary one. The roles are simple but quality social activities with cognitive benefits. Once they have a partner, do a buy-in (see chapter 21). Then, they are ready for one of the following tasks.

- **Clarifying the content:** When content is either tough, higher level, or obscurely written, this step is critical to use. Ask questions such as, "Can you rephrase that in your own words? What questions does that passage bring to you? How would you explain that to a student who knew nothing about this topic?"

- **Modeling teaching:** Students teach another how to do something, directions for an upcoming task, or how something works, unfolds, or develops.

- **Taking sides:** Give partners a topic, and have each pick a side. They get one minute to think through or write out a couple of talking points. Then, they argue their side (either pro or con on a topic). They can either switch sides or offer a rebuttal to their partner's arguments.

- **Taking a role:** Students take on a role (famous person in history, mathematician, leader, writer, scientist, or activist) and then add a bit of that person's character and make a policy speech (content summary). The other partner serves as a skeptic (or a reporter) and asks up to three questions.

- **Creating a quiz:** Two partners work together for nine minutes to create three questions each. When the time is up, ask them to remove

the easiest question from each list, so they have two left. Then, they
stand up and walk to find another twosome and trade quiz questions.
A third person can act as the arbiter of the quizzes.

When you get students up and moving, it invigorates blood flow and important chemicals like dopamine and noradrenaline. That's why any activity that lets students get up, walk, meet others, or even go outside is a good idea if it's done well. It is the activity that engages better brain chemicals (Gillberg et al., 1986).

Celebrating Small Whole-Class Victories

Set class goals and milestones (attendance, percentage of turned-in papers, or participation). Then, as the class gets close to the goal, ramp up the interest and the focus. This is the place to teach the value of keeping your macro goal in mind and focus on the moment. Micro goals keep morale high.

There's power in the timing and purpose of celebrating by managing student states with affirmations, celebrations, and emotional rewards. There are multiple ways to do this. For example, make the celebration a team activity. Teams will plan out their fifteen-second celebration and lead the whole class in it. Alternatively, you may create a class ritual for celebration by using a happy dance or rhythm-clap plus "We did it!" affirmations. The social side of this engagement strategy is key.

Quick Consolidation

In this chapter, we reinforced core strategies for community building in class. We want to have a classroom community of continuously engaged learners. When you create a community through activities, it fosters camaraderie and reduces inappropriate student behavior.

This chapter introduced a power tool: classroom rituals. I share these because I have used them with success for over thirty years. They are simple, free, and fun, and they work. Reciprocal teaching is another powerful way to engage students. Students love watching other students, and this creates a great sense of community. Finally, we end with whole-class celebrations.

If you already use these classroom activities, I invite you to sharpen them to get the most value. If you don't already use them, please give them a try. Your students are social, and engagement is the ticket to better learning. Which one are you willing to try out?

CHAPTER 23

LOCK IN THE ENGAGEMENT MINDSET

I am the first to admit that engagement was an "extra" when I began teaching. But soon I started seeing that I already engaged students when I did paired work. I already engaged students when I asked them to give each other feedback. In fact, I saw that I did many small things that added up to an active day for students. Truthfully, though, there were still students who were not always in the game.

Over time, I began to embrace the engagement mindset as a challenge. I started with making a list of all the engagement strategies I could use each week. Soon I learned to just pick and choose different activities from this list. I saw the benefits of continual engagement and became sold on a different mindset. The funny thing is that using the engagement strategies with a cheat sheet upfront gave me the confidence I needed. Now, when I do a day of staff development, I might use twenty-five strategies with no notes. The mindset is locked in.

Change the Narrative, Change Your Teaching

Many teachers who struggle may think engagement equals a loss of class control or is just too much work. Engagement needs to be your lifeblood that runs through the class every day, all day. High-performing teachers have embedded engagement so seamlessly into the teaching that there is no separation. The goal is relentless engagement, meaning you want to engage students every nine minutes or less. Will you always reach this goal? Sometimes not. There may be a reading, writing, or reflective assignment that lasts more than nine minutes. However, in other cases, plan to engage multiple times with any nine-minute chunk. What mindset narrative do you have? See figure 23.1.

You Are Your Mindset: Which Is Yours?

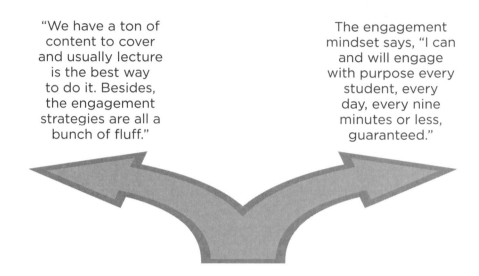

"We have a ton of content to cover and usually lecture is the best way to do it. Besides, the engagement strategies are all a bunch of fluff."

The engagement mindset says, "I can and will engage with purpose every student, every day, every nine minutes or less, guaranteed."

Figure 23.1: You are your mindset—the engagement mindset.

As we've seen, the engagement mindset is a specific way of thinking about your work. This mindset says three things. First, it says that engagement is worth doing, as in, the research is compelling. Second, the mindset says that it is doable using the strategies in this book. Finally, you can embed engagement so well into your teaching that they are inseparable. In short, the engagement mindset says that when you commit to engaging every student, every day, every nine minutes or less, learning is valuable, real, compelling, and doable.

Your ongoing teaching narrative is one of the single strongest predictors of student achievement. After reading each chapter, you'll notice that strong teachers are willing to change the narrative, both in their students' lives and their own. In the last few chapters, you have seen the power and simplicity of engaging activities. When you realize you have more of a choice in life and don't have to repeat less engaging classes, you can change your teaching story. You choose not what happens to you, but you choose how you respond to what happens to you. You choose to color your day with either emotions of positive energy, humility, grace, and confidence or to fill the day with complaints.

Fill in the following blanks with your name and a strategy from this mindset. Repeat the phrase daily until it's automatic.

"I, _____, am committing to building the engagement mindset in my students every single day. I will begin with one of the strategies mentioned, which is _____. I will continue this until I have mastery and it's automatic. At that point, I'll learn something new to foster student success."

Reflection and Decision

Take a moment and ask yourself a few questions before you finish up this part on engagement. For starters, ask yourself about the buy-in, mobility, and metabolic states of your students over a period of days and weeks. When things are going well, what percentage of the class is right in the palm of your hand? When you're struggling a bit, what percentage of your class is tuned out? About what percentage of your class do you feel is "with you" at any given moment? What are some choices you can make to help you and your students have a good day every day? Maybe you can make a list of those choices and plan a time for implementation.

Quick Consolidation

You've been introduced to several different ways to think of engagement. Your thinking should be, "I can engage any student anytime, at any level, and for any activity. I can do this every nine minutes or less all year long." That's the level of confidence you want. Over time, you'll have collected or developed enough strategies to back up that confidence by working with some new levels of engagement. Some benefits may turn out to be invisible to the untrained eye, but you'll know better. You'll have a classroom that has fewer problems and more joy. Plus, you'll influence more students to stay in school and graduate. That's a promise.

Epilogue

This epilogue begins with a brief consolidation. The reason is simple: there was plenty of content in this book, and it makes sense to sort it out. It also gives you an integration of the philosophy, mindset, and actions. These mindsets are critical because it is the presence of these in high-performing teachers (those who achieve at least two years of academic gains for each year in the classroom), who succeed with students from poverty, that warrants our attention. Finally, I'll ask for your decisions and action steps. As always, the choices are yours. You could put this book down and watch TV, take a walk, eat a bag of Cheetos, or take a nap, or you can do the hard work to begin the process of becoming extraordinary. I'm hoping you will choose the path of becoming extraordinary.

Listen: teaching is easy, but teaching *well* is tough. It is a consuming, soul-searching, and transformative process that may make for an awesome life at work. Otherwise, your job is, well, just a *job*. I am inviting you to invest the most energy in this chapter because it is about you. You know full well by now that it is possible to change students' attitudes, cognitive capacity, effort, and classroom behaviors. Each chapter has powerful, easy-to-implement factors you could take on to make miracles happen. Unfortunately, reading a book does not raise achievement in students, but it does start the process by planting seeds. This chapter will be all about converting the initial seeds of awareness into viable and lasting action steps.

Consider the mindsets and strategies throughout this book. I invite you to think differently about how your brain actually works and how changes affect it. It may even help you decide whether or not you should implement any of the strategies in this book. Before we move forward, let's consolidate what we have so far. The chapters have already introduced a series of core mindsets. Mindsets, as you know, are a way of thinking about something. They are a structure of premises, beliefs, and actions that run your life. Now is the time to reflect on each one of these. Are you willing to make the changes to help every student graduate career ready or job ready? Because if you are ready, these powerful mindsets will be an important part of the solution.

Changing Your Mindsets

There are four mindsets and narratives introduced in this book. On a separate piece of paper (or on your laptop or tablet), please write your thoughts about them. For example, do you buy into fully or halfway or reject the mindset? After each mindset, write how you have processed, planned, or responded to the challenges suggested. If you see places for improvement, how will you take action to make change happen? What will be the evidence procedure for tracking the changes you make? Consider also how you respond to change in regard to these four classroom mindsets: "Change is the new constant, especially in education, and it's only going to accelerate. I will grow and change myself."

1. The relational mindset says, "We are all connected in this life together. Always connect first as a person (and an ally) and as a teacher second."

2. The achievement mindset says, "I can build student effort, motivation, and attitudes to succeed. They are teachable skills."

3. The rich classroom climate mindset says, "I focus on what students need to succeed and build it into the learning and social environment every day."

4. The engagement mindset says, "I can and will engage with purpose every student, every day, every nine minutes or less, guaranteed."

For each of these mindsets, please respond to the following four questions or share with a colleague.

1. What has happened in the past in your classroom on this topic? (This speaks to your track record.)

2. Where do you see a place (if any) for making a change in regard to this mindset? (This speaks to your skills in reflection and the ability to be honest and actionable with yourself.)

3. For each change you'd like to make, what will be the evidence of success? How will you know when you succeed at it? (This speaks to your prediction skills and knowledge of your own limitations.)

4. When you have successfully implemented the changes from this activity, would you consider sharing your experiences (what you learned or did well) with colleagues? (This speaks to your social skills, school culture building, teamwork, and comfort with yourself.)

This powerful activity is an important part of learning, using formative evaluation (0.90 effect size), plus developing teacher clarity (0.75 effect size) and professional development and reflection (0.62 effect size; Hattie, 2009). To be exemplary, it takes a continual process of learning, reflection, decision making, planning, action steps, and feedback. This cycle of excellence will need to be repeated again and again for your whole career. Get used to it; it's the path of excellence.

Having Choices

You have heard multiple times in this book that your greatest power is the power of choice. You have a great deal of (but not total) influence over the input to your brain. You can choose to live in areas where the climate is cooler (versus warmer). (Yes, there are teaching jobs there.) You choose to spend time with certain friends or colleagues. You wear certain clothes that send messages about yourself. You choose what you eat, drink, and how much rest or exercise you get. You make decisions about having children or about being married. You decide to smoke, do drugs, or abuse medications. The truth is, you make countless choices every single day of your life. My question is, How is it working out so far?

Do you wake up every day and think, "My life is awesome—I love what I do, who I am with, and where we live"? If you paused before you answered that question, it's time to hold a conversation with yourself. Maybe your response was, "It's pretty good, but realistically, life's not exactly fair. It's not like I'm going to reach my own gutsy goal." This kind of conversation you have will directly affect your future and, along those same lines, what to do next with this book you've been reading.

These are truisms about the profession you're in. Many students do not come to school prepared to learn. Most teachers are underappreciated by their students, parents, and community as well as policymakers. Most schools lack the funding to do the things you wish could be done. Curriculum standards change every few years, often for the worse, not better. Many days of professional development are irrelevant and boring or a poor use of your time. I am sorry about that; life's not fair. Things change a lot at your school, often for no apparent good reason. You may feel like I'm stating the obvious, but I want you to know that I know the reality of your work. I've been a teacher myself, and I know it's tough, gritty work to get good at it.

Yes, life is simply not fair. Your job is likely different than what you signed up for. Like most teachers, you are likely an honest, good person that thinks fairness and equity are important. But some students get stressful, violent, or neglectful upbringings with no early enrichment, and they miss out on caring parental involvement or support. Life's not fair for them at all. Why the repetition of the phrase "Life's not fair"? Because most of the complaints I hear from teachers come from those with a negative mindset about the way things *should be*: "Things should be different than they are. Things should be fair, and I don't like it, and it's not fair!" Yes, you're right; life's not fair. As soon as you simply say it, you can start the process of lowering your stress. You see, as long as you cling to what should be (versus what is), you'll be stressed, frustrated, or disappointed over the gap.

Life is not about meeting the right person, finding the perfect situation, or having the perfect job. All of those can vaporize in a heartbeat (divorce, loss of a job, flood, sudden death, identity theft, and so on). Life is about creating and growing into the person who can constantly create or recreate the life you want. No matter where you live, no matter the job you do, you can foster the attitudes, skills, passion, and mindsets that lead to who you become. You may become so awesome that you can enjoy life on your own terms, but you have got to start with the truth.

Over ninety years before Nobel Laureate Daniel Kahneman (as cited in Brockman, 2012) talked about what makes for a full life (connecting with people, having meaningful work, making progress, and having control over what you're doing), playwright George Bernard Shaw (1903) said:

> This is the true joy in life, the being used for a purpose recognized by yourself as a mighty one; the being thoroughly worn out before you are thrown on the scrap heap; the being a force of Nature instead of a feverish selfish little clod of ailments and grievances complaining that the world will not devote itself to making you happy. (p. 15)

What Shaw is saying is simple and quite profound: whatever you decide to do in life, throw yourself into it 100 percent, and stop expecting others to make you happy. Naturally, this applies to you as you finish up this book.

Answering Final Questions to Elicit Change

Some of the questions in this section may be a bit uncomfortable, but all of them are relevant. One of these questions may trigger the answer that could change your life. Now, maybe you think your life is awesome, and there's no need for change. If your students' scores are high, we all love you, but if there are some gaps, I might respond, "For your students to change, you'll have to go first." Nothing, and I mean that word with all its connotations (*zero, zip, nada*, absolutely *nil*), will get better at school unless there are shifts in your mindsets and actions. Let's continue your thinking with the following questions.

- When you were in school, which teachers did you work hardest for? Which teachers motivated you to pay attention, learn, work hard, and complete assignments? What traits or qualities did they show? What could you do that is similar?

- When you read about some of the high-performing teachers in this book, how did you feel? Did you feel awestruck and inspired, or did you feel threatened and dismissive of their success?

- When you think of your profession, do you feel like you just need to show up and get through it? Do you feel the urgency that collectively, we need to make changes now?

- When you look at your own test scores, do you see them as the upper limits of student capacity? Do you now see that students can be taught in ways that build cognitive capacity so they can improve? Are you willing to do that?

- When you see students who seem lethargic, do you point fingers at them and say, "What's wrong with you? Sit up, and get to work!" Do you recall that effort is teachable and there are things you can do to bring out more effort in students?

Each question speaks to your mindsets. Just reading this book doesn't mean that you changed anything. True positive change comes from the development of true expertise in a life filled with purposeful workplace practice and integration of high-level personal beliefs. You'll have to be the change first before you see it in your students.

Reflection and self-change are critical for becoming a great teacher. I'm hoping that capacity for change is a core part of your character. It's part of what makes us all human. If you're the same teacher who walked through the door into the classroom this year as you were last year, you're in trouble, and your students are too. Many teachers expect students to change when, inside, they are the same teacher, doing the same thing year after year. If you want students to be different and better, you'll have to be different and better.

You'll need to try out powerful new ways of teaching, with new effort and a new attitude. Fortunately, you do not need to work more hours. As noted previously, high performers work fewer hours per week than low-performing teachers (Jensen, 2014). If you are not upgrading your professional skill sets and changing yourself constantly, how can you realistically expect your own students to change?

As you grow up, you're told that the world is a certain way. You learn who is smart, reliable, hardworking, and trustworthy. You also learn from school colleagues whether or not you can succeed with the students at your school. They had already created a school culture when you arrived. Over time, it's easy to develop a fixed mindset of "Here's how your students are, how your school is, and ultimately, how the world is." If they tell you "Those students will always struggle," do you believe what others say?

I am hoping that by reading this book you want the truth: students can change if teachers change first. Allow yourself to change often, and be purposeful about it. When you continually upgrade your attitudes and skill sets, you'll be a different person and better teacher. That one decision you make—the decision to allow yourself to grow, to take savvy risks, and to be different—can make all the difference between whether your students struggle this year or whether you have the greatest professional year of your life. What will it be?

You see, once you learn that the world waits for people who are willing to poke it, probe it, expand it, and rethink it and shake the boundaries, then you understand why miracles can happen. You can see how the seas parted for people who thought differently: such as Steve Jobs (cofounder of Apple), Jay Z (media mogul), Sonia Sotomayor (Supreme Court justice), Rosa Parks (civil rights activist), Jeff Bezos (founder of Amazon), Mark Zuckerberg (founder of Facebook), Sally Ride (first American woman in space), and others who simply said, "Why not?" None of these made excuses; they just said, "How can I make it happen?"

You see, there are two types of teachers. One points to a struggling student and says, "Bless his (or her) heart. It's a shame; he's just like his daddy" or "What's wrong with this student? He just sits there like a lump. No motivation or interest in learning!" However, the other teacher says, "I know the deck is stacked. I know that he or she has had a tough home life. But this student *will not* fail on my watch. Nothing is impossible and he (or she) *will* graduate."

Once you learn that you don't have to be a victim or stay the same, life is different. You see, wash, rinse, and repeat are easy. Your brain and body are designed to preserve habits, but is what you're doing *really* working? Because, if things are not working, it's time for change. Once you recognize you have the power to change yourself any time you want, you'll never be the same again. If you're waiting for the government or the school district to make your life better, how's that working out so far? If feeling comfortable in your job and doing more of the same is more important to you than helping your students succeed, put this book down, and start a job search. If you came into teaching because you thought you could make a difference and change lives, welcome aboard. The choice is yours. Are you prepared to make the right choices? See figure E.1.

Figure E.2 provides a checklist with the mindsets strategies throughout the book. Are you prepared to make the changes for yourself and your students? As you go down the list, be brutally honest. Ask yourself, "Could I use this, or do I already have this in place?" Create a list of favorites. Once you have your own list, prioritize it, using your own criteria. You might consider criteria such as timing (when is the best time of the school year to start this?), complexity (how hard will it be to master?), instructional tools (does this replace something I already do or not?), or collaboration (what are my colleagues doing?). Once you're ready, set your gutsy goals and micro goals. Implement, adjust, celebrate, and add a new strategy to keep getting better.

You Are Your Mindset: Which Is Yours?

"It's not my fault. We teachers get kicked around, plus the parents and students don't care. No wonder everybody is stressed and students drop out."

"My greatest power is the power of choice. I have a great deal of influence over how I run my own brain. I remember this every day: I have a choice."

Figure E.1: You are your mindset—preparing to make choices.

Student Mindsets

Check the boxes where you can upgrade your students' brains.

Relational Mindset

- ☐ Personalize the learning.
- ☐ Connect everyone for success.
- ☐ Show empathy.

Achievement Mindset

- ☐ Set gutsy goals.
- ☐ Have the right attitude.
- ☐ Give fabulous feedback.
- ☐ Persist with grit.

Rich Classroom Climate Mindset

- ☐ Engage voice and vision.
- ☐ Set safe classroom norms.
- ☐ Foster academic optimism.

Figure E.2: Checklist for changing mindsets.

continued on next page ⇨

Engagement Mindset

    ☐ Engage for maintenance and stress.

    ☐ Engage for setup and buy-in.

    ☐ Engage to build community.

Getting Started With Students

    • The specific strategies I will begin to use are:

    • I'll start doing this beginning:

    • I will assess progress for my feedback on:

    • I plan to have this strategy completely automated by:

Personal Strategies

Check the boxes where you can upgrade your own brain.

    ☐ **Change:** Change is a constant, especially in education, and it's only going to accelerate. I will grow and change myself.

    ☐ **The relational mindset:** We are all connected. Always connect as a person first (and an ally) and as a teacher second.

    ☐ **The achievement mindset:** I can build student effort, motivation, and attitudes to succeed. They are all teachable skills.

    ☐ **The rich classroom climate mindset:** I focus on what students need to succeed and build it into the learning and social environment every day.

    ☐ **The engagement mindset:** I can and will engage with purpose, every student, every day, every nine minutes, or less, guaranteed.

    ☐ **Choice:** My greatest power is the power of choice. I have a great deal of influence over how I run my own brain. I remember this every day: I have a choice.

    ☐ Change the narrative.

    ☐ Destress your brain.

    ☐ Create better rewards for yourself.

    ☐ Make a plan.

Getting Started

    • The specific mindset I will begin to use is:

    • I'll start doing this beginning:

    • I will assess progress for my feedback on:

    • I plan to have this strategy completely automated by:

*Visit **go.solution-tree.com/instruction** for a free reproducible version of this figure.*

We have to face up to the reality: the same old mindsets and the same old strategies are not working. You might not *want* to hear this, but you *need* to hear this: if students from poverty are different, whose job is it to do the adjusting? Students are only in school because they have to be there; it's the law, and their friends are there.

The school staff works by choice, however; they are educated, trained, and paid professionals whose job is to help prepare students for life after school. If a student can't read by third grade, how is that his or her fault? If the student is underperforming in mathematics, since when is that his or her fault? If students from poverty have cognitive and behavioral challenges, who is getting paid to help students read, think, calculate, write, and behave appropriately? We can point fingers at the students all we want, but how does that build the next generation?

Right now the percentage of students from families who are poor and of color have a coin flip's chance (50 percent) of graduating from high school (Seastrom, Hoffman, Chapman, & Stillwell, 2005). How long do you think we (collectively) can allow that to happen? If we don't help students graduate job ready and college ready, in twenty years you won't recognize the country you live in. Please help students succeed. Remember, you do have a choice to make. The next time you hear another teacher complain say, "I hear your frustration. Now what are you going to do about that problem to help your student graduate?"

Quick Consolidation

Thank you for making this journey. I know your work is hard. I know there are obstacles with silly rules and crazy standards. I know the pay is unfair. I know that conditions are often suboptimal. What is also true is that the students need you very, very badly to help them get an education every day. The way to make this book a part of you is to begin today. Do something, and use repetition until it's automatic. The better you get, the more students will graduate job and college ready. Focus on the rich teaching difference (relationships, rigor, and relevance). Now, that makes *me* happy and hopefully you too. Thank you again for the kindness of your attention and the work you do. Now, go prep your new lesson plan!

Fill in the following blanks with your name, a mindset, and strategies from this book. Repeat the phrase daily until it's automatic.

"I, _____, am committing to building a monthly mindset with my students every single day. I will begin with one of the mindsets mentioned, which is _____, and use the following strategies _____. I will continue this until I have mastery and it's automatic. At that point, I'll learn something new to foster student success."

Create a simple system to nudge yourself toward your goals every day. I recommend answering the following five questions (at your desk) each day before leaving your classroom. Why? Because change is hard. We typically underestimate the difficulties and environmental prompts and intrusions that distract us. Make your system a habit just like brushing your teeth.

1. Did I do my best to foster optimism and gratitude today?
2. Did I do my best to make this work relevant to both me and my students?
3. Did I do my best to foster stronger personal relationships?
4. Did I do my best to fully engage and help others?
5. Did I do my best to grow personally and professionally today?

With your structure, you can make miracles happen in your life. Scattered, random positive things in your classroom will have little lasting effect. But make one small change, take one micro step, or try a mini attitude booster, and you'll see miracles happen over time. Can you start today?

Appendix
Resources for Getting Started

Visit **go.solution-tree/instruction** to access direct links to these resources.

Boys Hope Girls Hope (www.boyshopegirlshope.org): Boys Hope Girls Hope is a scholarship program connecting a network of fifteen U.S. and three Latin American academic sites that provides middle school students with academic support through college and career entry.

Brain-Based Learning (www.brainbasedlearning.net): Brain-Based Learning links practical strategies and powerful research to understand the brain and learning. Using its helpful resources, teachers will discover how to make their teaching more purposeful to reach a great number of students.

Jensen Learning (www.jensenlearning.com): Jensen Learning provides workshops, books, DVDs, and podcasts on succeeding with students from poverty.

Jungle Memory (http://junglememory.com): Jungle Memory provides skill building for attention and working memory.

Minds Matter (http://mindsmatter.org): Minds Matter advises low-income high school students. Working with a team of mentees, students in the program participate in a three-year curriculum to prepare for college.

Read to Them (http://readtothem.org/our-programs/one-school-one-book/join-osob): Read to Them is a nonprofit organization promoting family literacy in every home.

Scientific Learning (www.scilearn.com): Scientific Learning provides optimal brain-changing tools to help students who struggle with reading.

Spark (http://sparkprogram.org): With Spark, seventh- and eighth-grade students have a chance for a ten-week career apprenticeship.

SuperCamp (www.supercamp.com): SuperCamp is an academic enrichment program for struggling students in grades 5–12.

10 Minute Lesson Plans (www.10minutelessonplans.com): 10 Minute Lesson Plans offers a research-based program for building short, effective lesson plans.

YouthBuild (www.youthbuild.org): YouthBuild offers career advice for low-income dropouts. Participants learn construction skills while building affordable housing.

References and Resources

Adcock, R. A., Thangavel, A., Whitfield-Gabrieli, S., Knutson, B., & Gabrieli, J. D. (2006). Reward-motivated learning: Mesolimbic activation precedes memory formation. *Neuron, 50*(3), 507–17.

Adelabu, D. H. (2007). Time perspective and school membership as correlates to academic achievement among African American adolescents. *Adolescence, 42*(167), 525–538.

Allen, J. P., McElhaney, K. B., Kuperminc, G. P., & Jodl, K. M. (2004). Stability and change in attachment security across adolescence. *Child Development, 75*(6), 1792–1805.

Alloway, T. P., & Alloway, R. G. (2010). Investigating the predictive roles of working memory and IQ in academic attainment. *Journal of Experimental Child Psychology, 106*(1), 20–29.

Almeida, D. M., Neupert, S. D., Banks, S. R., & Serido, J. (2005). Do daily stress processes account for socioeconomic health disparities? *Journals of Gerontology: Series B, 60*, 34–39.

Altucher, J. (2012). *40 alternatives to college.* Seattle, WA: CreateSpace.

American Institute for Economic Research Staff. (2012). The everyday price index. *American Institute for Economic Research Economic Bulletin, LII.* Accessed at www.aier.org/sites /default/files/Files/Documents/Research/3631/EB201202.pdf on May 22, 2015.

Amodio, D. M., Harmon-Jones, E., Devine, P. G., Curtin, J. J., Hartley, S. L., & Covert, A. E. (2004). Neural signals for the detection of unintentional race bias. *Psychological Science, 15*(2), 88–93.

Appleton, J. J., Christenson, S. L., & Furlong, M. J. (2008). Student engagement with school: Critical conceptual and methodological issues of the construct. *Psychology in the Schools, 45*, 369–386.

Arakaki, M. (2010, November 4). *Mr. Irish's classroom football theme* [Video file]. Accessed at www.youtube.com/watch?v=Y6kp11hMTIk on May 22, 2015.

Aydin, K., Ucar, A., Oguz, K. K., Okur, O. O., Agayev, A., Unal, Z., et al. (2007). Increased gray matter density in the parietal cortex of mathematicians: A voxel-based morphometry study. *American Journal of Neuroradiology, 28*(10), 1859–1864.

Azer, S. A. (2011). Learning surface anatomy: Which learning approach is effective in an integrated PBL curriculum? *Medical Teacher, 33*(1), 78–80.

Banks, J., Cochran-Smith, M., Moll, L., Richert, A., Zeichner, K., LePage, P., et al. (2005). Teaching diverse learners. In L. Darling-Hammond & J. Bransford (Eds.), *Preparing teachers for a changing world: What teachers should learn and be able to do* (pp. 232–274). San Francisco: Jossey-Bass.

Bastian, B., Kuppens, P., De Roover, K., & Diener, E. (2014). Is valuing positive emotion associated with life satisfaction? *Emotion, 14*(4), 639–645.

Baumeister, R. F., Bratslavsky, E., Finkenauer, C., & Vohs, K. D. (2001). Bad is stronger than good. *Review of General Psychology, 5*(4), 323–370.

Baumeister, R. F., & Leary, M. R. (1995). The need to belong: Desire for interpersonal attachments as a fundamental human motivation. *Psychological Bulletin, 117*(3), 497–529.

Belfield, C. R., Levin, H. M., & Rosen, R. (2012, January). *The economic value of opportunity youth.* Washington, DC: Civic Enterprises. Accessed at www.serve.gov/sites/default/files /ctools/econ_value_opportunity_youth.pdf on May 3, 2014.

Berns, G. S., Blaine, K., Prietula, M. J., & Pye, B. E. (2013). Short- and long-term effects of a novel on connectivity in the brain. *Brain Connectivity, 3*(6), 590–600.

Best, J. R. (2010). Effects of physical activity on children's executive function: Contributions of experimental research on aerobic exercise. *Developmental Review, 30*(4), 331–351.

Bhullar, N., Schutte, N. S., & Malouff, J. M. (2013). The nature of well-being: the roles of hedonic and eudaimonic processes and trait emotional intelligence. *The Journal of Psychology: Interdisciplinary and Applied, 147*(1), 1–16.

Biffle, C. (2013). *Whole brain teaching for challenging kids.* San Bernardino, CA: Whole Brain Teaching.

Black, P., & Wiliam, D. (1998). Inside the black box: Raising standards through classroom assessment. *Phi Delta Kappan, 80*(2), 139–148.

Blackwell, L. S., Trzesniewski, K. H., & Dweck, C. S. (2007). Implicit theories of intelligence predict achievement across an adolescent transition: A longitudinal study and an intervention. *Child Development, 78*(1), 246–263.

Blake, D. T., Heiser, M. A., Caywood, M., & Merzenich, M. M. (2006). Experience-dependent adult cortical plasticity requires cognitive association between sensation and reward. *Neuron, 52*(2), 371–381.

Bogdan, R., & Pizzagalli, D. A. (2006). Acute stress reduces reward responsiveness: Implications for depression. *Biological Psychiatry, 60*(10), 1147–1154.

Bolte, A., Goschkey, T., & Kuhl, J. (2003). Emotion and intuition: Effects of positive and negative mood on implicit judgments of semantic coherence. *Psychological Science, 14*(5), 416–421.

Bouffard, S. (2014). A new role for guidance counselors. *Harvard Education Letter, 30*(6). Accessed at http://hepg.org/hel-home/issues/volume-30,-number-6/helarticle/a-new -role-for-guidance-counselors on May 22, 2015.

Boushey, H., Bernstein, J., & Mishel, L. (2002). *The state of working America 2002–03.* Washington, DC: Economic Policy Institute.

Boykin, A. W., Tyler, K. M., Watkins-Lewis, K., & Kizzie, K. (2006). Culture in the sanctioned classroom practices of elementary school teachers serving low-income African American students. *Journal of Education for Students Placed at Risk, 11*(2), 161–173.

Brennan, T. (2004). *The transmission of affect.* Ithaca, NY: Cornell University Press.

Bridgeland, J. M., DiIulio, J. J., Jr., & Morison, K. B. (2006, March). *The silent epidemic: Perspectives of high school dropouts.* Washington, DC: Civic Enterprises. Accessed at www .ignitelearning.com/pdf/TheSilentEpidemic3-06FINAL.pdf on February 4, 2013.

Brockman, J. (Ed.). (2012). *This will make you smarter: New scientific concepts to improve your thinking.* New York: Harper Perennial.

Brody, G. H., Lei, M. K., Chen, E., & Miller, G. E. (2014). Neighborhood poverty and allostatic load in African American youth. *Pediatrics, 134*(5), 1362–1368.

Bruckheimer, J. (Producer), Oman, C. (Producer), & Washington, D. (Director). (2001). *Remember the Titans* [Motion picture]. United States: Walt Disney Home Video.

Brummelman, E., Thomaes, S., Overbeek, G., Orobio de Castro, B., van den Hout, M. A., & Bushman, B. J. (2014). On feeding those hungry for praise: Person praise backfires in children with low self-esteem. *Journal of Experimental Psychology: General, 143*(1), 9–14.

Budde, H., Voelcker-Rehage, C., Pietrabyk-Kendziorra, S., Ribeiro, P., & Tidow, G. (2008). Acute coordinative exercise improves attentional performance in adolescents. *Neuroscience Letters, 441*(2), 219–223.

Buonomano, D. V. (2014). Neural dynamics based timing in the subsecond to seconds range. In H. Merchang & V. de Lafuente (Eds.), *Neurobiology of interval timing: Advances in experimental medicine and biology 829* (pp. 101–117). New York: Springer.

Burgess, D. (2012). *Teach like a pirate: Increase student engagement, boost your creativity, and transform your life as an educator.* San Diego, CA: Dave Burgess Consulting.

Butler-Barnes, S. T., Williams, T. T., & Chavous, T. M. (2012). Racial pride and religiosity among African American boys: Implications for academic motivation and achievement. *Journal of Youth and Adolescence, 41*(4), 486–498.

Caldwell, C. H., Zimmerman, M. A., Bernat, D. H., Sellers, R. M., & Notaro, P. C. (2002). Racial identity, maternal support, and psychological distress among African American adolescents. *Child Development, 73*(4), 1322–1336.

Carlson, C. R., Collins, F. L., Jr., Nitz, A. J., Sturgis, E. T., & Rogers, J. L. (1990). Muscle stretching as an alternative relaxation training procedure. *Journal of Behavior Therapy and Experimental Psychiatry, 21*(1), 29–38.

Carney, D. R., Cuddy, A. J. C., & Yap, A. J. (2010). Power posing: Brief nonverbal displays affect neuroendocrine levels and risk tolerance. *Psychological Science, 21*(10), 1363–1368.

Catalino, L. I., & Fredrickson, B. L. (2011). A Tuesday in the life of a flourisher: The role of positive emotional reactivity in optimal mental health. *Emotion, 11*(4), 938–950.

Catt, M. (Producer), & Kendrick, A. (Director). (2006). *Facing the giants* [Motion picture]. United States: Samuel Goldwyn Films.

Ceballo, R. (2004). From barrios to Yale: The role of parenting strategies in Latino families. *Hispanic Journal of Behavioral Sciences, 26*(2), 171–186.

Ceci, S. J., & Williams, W. M. (1997). Schooling, intelligence, and income. *American Psychologist, 52*(10), 1051–1058.

Centre for Confidence and Well-Being. (n.d.). *Glasgow University mindset research.* Accessed at www.centreforconfidence.co.uk/information.php?p=cGlkPTE1NQ== on May 22, 2015.

Chan, C. S., Rhodes, J. E., Howard, W. J., Lowe, S. R., Schwartz, S. E., & Herrera, C. (2013). Pathways of influence in school-based mentoring: The mediating role of parent and teacher relationships. *Journal of School Psychology, 51*(1), 129–142.

Chetty, R., Friedman, J. N., Hilger, N., Saez, E., Schanzenbach, D. W., & Yagan, D. (2011). How does your kindergarten classroom affect your earnings?: Evidence from Project STAR. *Quarterly Journal of Economics, 126*(4), 1593–1660.

ChildStats. (2015). *America's children: Key national indicators of well-being, 2015—Child poverty.* Accessed at www.childstats.gov/americaschildren/eco1.asp on October 14, 2015.

Choi, J., Jeong, B., Rohan, M. L., Polcari, A. M., & Teicher, M. H. (2009). Preliminary evidence for white matter tract abnormalities in young adults exposed to parental verbal abuse. *Biological Psychiatry, 65*(3), 227–234.

Chung-Do, J., Filibeck, K., Goebert, D. A., Arakawa, G., Fraser, D., Laboy, J., et al. (2013). Understanding students' perceptions of a high school course designed to enhance school connectedness. *Journal of School Health, 83*(7), 478–484.

Cimpian, A., Arce, H.-M., Markman, E. M., & Dweck, C. S. (2007). Subtle linguistic cues affect children's motivation. *Psychological Science, 18*(4), 314–316.

Coe, D. P., Pivarnik, J. M., Womack, C. J., Reeves, M. J., & Malina, R. M. (2006). Effect of physical education and activity levels on academic achievement in children. *Medicine and Science in Sports and Exercise, 38*(8), 1515–1519.

Coe, R. (2002, September). *It's the effect size, stupid: What effect size is and why it is important.* Paper presented at the Annual Conference of the British Educational Research Association, University of Exeter, England.

Cohen, G. L., Garcia, J., Purdie-Vaughns, V., Apfel, N., & Brzustoski, P. (2009). Recursive processes in self-affirmation: Intervening to close the minority achievement gap. *Science, 324*(5925), 400–403.

Cohler, B. J. (1980). Personal narrative and life course. In P. Baltes & O. G. Brim Jr. (Eds.), *Life span development and behavior* (Vol. 4, pp. 205–241). New York: Academic Press.

Coller, R. J., & Kuo, A. A. (2014). Youth development through mentorship: A Los Angeles school-based mentorship program among Latino children. *Journal of Community Health, 39*(2), 316–321.

Commission on Children at Risk. (2003). *Hardwired to connect: The new scientific case for authoritative communities.* New York: Institute for American Values.

Cook, J. E., Purdie-Vaughns, V., Garcia, J., & Cohen, G. L. (2012). Chronic threat and contingent belonging: Protective benefits of values affirmation on identity development. *Journal of Personality and Social Psychology, 102*(3), 479–496.

Cook, S. W., Mitchell, Z., & Goldin-Meadow, S. (2008). Gesturing makes learning last. *Cognition, 106*(2), 1047–1058.

Conzemius, A. E., & O'Neill, J. (2014). *The handbook for SMART school teams: Revitalizing best practices for collaboration.* Bloomington, IN: Solution Tree Press.

Coplan, J. D., Andrews, M. W., Rosenblum, L. A., Owens, M. J., Friedman, S., Gorman, J. M.,et al. (1996). Persistent elevations of cerebrospinal fluid concentrations of corticotropin-releasing factor in adult nonhuman primates exposed to early-life stressors: Implications for the pathophysiology of mood and anxiety disorders. *Proceedings of the National Academy of Sciences of the United States of America, 93*, 1619–1623.

Covey, S. R. (2013). *The 7 habits of highly effective people: Powerful lessons in personal change.* New York: Simon & Schuster.

De La Paz, S. (2005). Teaching historical reasoning and argumentative writing in culturally and academically diverse middle school classrooms. *Journal of Educational Psychology, 97*(2), 139–158.

DeNavas-Walt, C., Proctor, B. D., & Smith, J. C. (2011). *Income, poverty, and health insurance coverage in the United States: 2010.* (Current Population Reports). Washington, DC: U.S. Government Printing Office.

Dexter, C. A., Wong, K., Stacks, A. M., Beeghly, M., & Barnett, D. (2013). Parenting and attachment among low-income African American and Caucasian preschoolers. *Journal of Family Psychology, 27*(4), 629–638.

Dharmadhikari, A. S. (2013). Six degrees of separation: Use of social network analysis to better understand outbreaks of nosocomial transmission of extensively drug-resistant tuberculosis. *Journal of Infectious Diseases, 207*(1), 1–3.

Doan, S. N., & Evans, G. W. (2011). Maternal responsiveness moderates the relationship between allostatic load and working memory. *Development and Psychopathology, 23*(3), 873–880.

Douglas-Hall, A., & Chau, M. (2007). *Most low-income parents are employed.* New York: National Center for Children in Poverty.

Draganski, B., Gaser, C., Busch, V., Schuierer, G., Bogdahn, U., & May, A. (2004) Neuroplasticity: Changes in grey matter induced by training. *Nature, 427*(6972), 311–312.

Duckworth, A. L., Kirby, T. A., Oettingen, G., & Gollwitzer, A. (2013). From fantasy to action: Mental contrasting with implementation intentions (MCII) improves academic performance in children. *Social Psychological and Personality Science, 4*(6), 745–753.

Duckworth, A. L., Peterson, C., Matthews, M. D., & Kelly, D. R. (2007). Grit: Perseverance and passion for long-term goals. *Journal of Personality and Social Psychology, 92*(6), 1087–1101.

Duckworth, A. L., Quinn, P. D., Lynam, D. R., Loeber, R., & Stouthamer-Loeber, M. (2011). Role of test motivation in intelligence testing. *Proceedings of the National Academy of Sciences of the United States of America, 108*(19), 7716–7720.

Duckworth, A. L., Quinn, P. D., & Seligman, M. E. P. (2009). Positive predictors of teacher effectiveness. *Journal of Positive Psychology, 4*(6), 540–547.

Dunning, D. L., Holmes, J., & Gathercole, S. E. (2013). Does working memory training lead to generalized improvements in children with low working memory? A randomized controlled trial. *Developmental Science, 16*(6), 915–925.

Dusek, J. A., Otu, H. H., Wohlhueter, A. L., Bhasin, M., Zerbini, L. F., Joseph, M. G., et al. (2008). Genomic counter-stress changes induced by the relaxation response. *PLoS ONE, 3*(7), e2576.

Duyme, M., Dumaret, A.-C., & Tomkiewicz, S. (1999). How can we boost IQs of "dull children"?: A late adoption study. *Proceedings of the National Academy of Sciences of the United States of America, 96*(15), 8790–8794.

Dweck, C. S. (1999). *Self-theories: Their role in motivation, personality, and development.* Lillington, NC: Edwards Brothers.

Dweck, C. S. (2002). The development of ability conceptions. In A. Wigfield & J. S. Eccles (Eds.), *Development of achievement motivation* (pp. 57–88). New York: Academic Press.

Dweck, C. S. (2008). *Mindset: The new psychology of success (how we can learn to fulfill our potential).* New York: Ballantine Books.

Eamon, M. K. (2001). The effects of poverty on children's socioemotional development: An ecological systems analysis. *Social Work, 46*(3), 256–266.

Edcoogle. (2014, September 24). *5 amazing kids who changed the world. This is inspirational.* Accessed at www.edcoogle.com/blog/2014/09/5-amazing-kids-changed-world-inspirational on October 21, 2015.

Eichenlaub, J. B., Ruby, P., & Morlet, D. (2012). What is the specificity of the response to the own first-name when presented as a novel in a passive oddball paradigm?: An ERP study. *Brain Research, 1447,* 65–78.

Eldridge, B., Galea, M., McCoy, A., Wolfe, R., & Graham, H. K. (2003). Uptime normative values in children aged 8 to 15 years. *Developmental Medicine and Child Neurology, 45*(3), 189–193.

Elliot, A. J., & Dweck, C. S. (Eds.). (2005). *Handbook of competence and motivation.* New York: Guilford Press.

Elliott, E. S., & Dweck, C. S. (1988). Goals: An approach to motivation and achievement. *Journal of Personality and Social Psychology, 54*(1), 5–12.

Engel de Abreu, P. M., Abreu, N., Nikaedo, C. C., Puglisi, M. L., Tourinho, C. J., Miranda, M. C., et al. (2014). Executive functioning and reading achievement in school: A study of Brazilian children assessed by their teachers as "poor readers." *Frontiers in Psychology, 10,* 550.

Engineer, N. D., Engineer, C. T., Reed, A. C., Pandya, P. K., Jakkamsetti, V., Moucha, R., et al. (2012). Inverted-U function relating cortical plasticity and task difficulty. *Neuroscience, 205,* 81–90.

Evans, G. W., & English, K. (2002). The environment of poverty: Multiple stressor exposure, psychophysiological stress, and socioemotional adjustment. *Child Development, 73*(4), 1238–1248.

Evans, G. W., & Kim, P. (2007). Childhood poverty and health: Cumulative risk exposure and stress dysregulation. *Psychological Science, 18*(11), 953–957.

Evans, G. W., & Schamberg, M. A. (2009). Childhood poverty, chronic stress, and adult working memory. *Proceedings of the National Academy of Sciences of the United States of America, 106*(16), 6545–6549.

Farr, S. (2010). *Teaching as leadership: The highly effective teacher's guide to closing the achievement gap.* San Francisco: Jossey-Bass.

Federal Interagency Forum on Child and Family Statistics. (2011). *America's children: Key national indicators of well-being, 2011.* Washington, DC: U.S. Government Printing Office. Accessed at www.childstats.gov/pdf/ac2011/ac_11.pdf on May 22, 2015.

Finerman, W. (Producer), Starkey, S. (Producer), Tisch, S. (Producer), & Zemeckis, R. (Director). (1994). *Forrest Gump* [Motion picture]. United States: Paramount Pictures.

Fishman, S. (2012). *The first five: Maximizing the opening minutes of class.* Accessed at http://tntp.org/assets/documents/TNTP_FishmanPrizeSeries_2012.pdf on October 22, 2015.

Fredrickson, B. L., & Branigan, C. A. (2005). Positive emotions broaden the scope of attention and thought-action repertoires. *Cognition and Emotion, 19*(3), 313–332.

Fredrickson, B. L., Grewen, K. M., Coffey, K. A., Algoe, S. B., Firestine, A. M., Arevalo, J. M. G., et al. (2013). A functional genomic perspective on human well-being. *Proceedings of the National Academy of Sciences of the United States of America, 110*(33), 13684–13689.

Fredrickson, B. L., & Losada, M. F. (2005). Positive affect and the complex dynamics of human flourishing. *American Psychologist, 60*(7), 678–686.

Fry, R. (2013, August). *A rising share of young adults live in their parents' home.* Washington, DC: Pew Research Center. Accessed at www.pewsocialtrends.org/files/2013/07/SDT -millennials-living-with-parents-07-2013.pdf on May 2, 2014.

Gabe, T. (2010, April). *Poverty in the United States: 2008.* Washington, DC: Congressional Research Service. Accessed at http://assets.opencrs.com/rpts/RL33069_20100421.pdf on May 22, 2015.

Galla, B. M., Plummer, B. D., White, R. E., Meketon, D., D'Mello, S. K., & Duckworth, A. L. (2014). The Academic Diligence Task (ADT): Assessing individual differences in effort on tedious but important schoolwork. *Contemporary Educational Psychology, 39*(4), 314–325.

Garner, P. W. (1996). The relations of emotional role taking, affective/moral attributions, and emotional display rule knowledge to low-income school-age children's social competence. *Journal of Applied Developmental Psychology, 17*(1), 19–36.

Gay, G. (2010). *Culturally responsive teaching: Theory, research, and practice* (2nd ed.). New York: Teachers College Press.

Gazzaniga, M. S. (1998). *The mind's past.* Los Angeles: University of California Press.

Getahun, D., Jacobsen, S. J., Fassett, M. J., Chen, W., Demissie, K., & Rhoads, G. G. (2013). Recent trends in childhood attention-deficit/hyperactivity disorder. *Journal of the American Medical Association Pediatrics, 167*(3), 282–288.

Gillberg, M., Anderzén, I., Åkerstedt, T., & Sigurdson, K. (1986). Urinary catecholamine responses to basic types of physical activity. *European Journal of Applied Physiology and Occupational Physiology, 55*(6), 575–578.

Glaze, L. E., & Parks, E. (2012, November). *Correctional populations in the United States, 2011.* Washington, DC: Bureau of Justice Statistics. Accessed at www.bjs.gov/content /pub/pdf/cpus11.pdf on May 22, 2015.

Goldin-Meadow, S., Cook, S. W., & Mitchell, Z. A. (2009). Gesturing gives children new ideas about math. *Psychological Science, 20*(3), 267–272.

Gollnick, D. M., & Chinn, P. (2013). *Multicultural education in a pluralistic society.* Boston: Pearson.

Gonzalez-Mena, J., & Pulido-Tobiassen, D. (1999). *Teaching diversity: A place to begin.* Accessed at www.scholastic.com/teachers/article/teaching-diversity-place-begin-0 on October 14, 2015.

Good, C., Aronson, J., & Inzlicht, M. (2003). Improving adolescents' standardized test performance: An intervention to reduce the effects of stereotype threat. *Journal of Applied Developmental Psychology, 24*(6), 645–662.

Goodyear, D. (2009, October 26). Man of extremes: The return of James Cameron. *The New Yorker.* Accessed at www.newyorker.com/reporting/2009/10/26/091026fa_fact_goodyear on October 14, 2015.

Gorski, P. (2008). The myth of the culture of poverty. *Educational Leadership, 65*(7), 32–36.

Graham, S., & Perin, D. (2007). *Writing next: Effective strategies to improve writing of adolescents in middle and high schools.* Washington, DC: Alliance for Excellent Education.

Grant, H., & Dweck, C. S. (2003). Clarifying achievement goals and their impact. *Journal of Personality and Social Psychology, 85*(3), 541–553.

Green, C. S., & Bavelier, D. (2008). Exercising your brain: A review of human brain plasticity and training-induced learning. *Psychology and Aging, 23*(4), 692–701.

Hafen, C. A., Allen, J. P., Mikami, A. Y., Gregory, A., Hamre, B., & Pianta, R. C. (2012). The pivotal role of adolescent autonomy in secondary school classrooms. *Journal of Youth and Adolescence, 41*(3), 245–255.

Halassa, M. M., Chen, Z., Wimmer, R. D., Brunetti, P. M., Zhao, S., Zikopoulos, B., et al. (2014). State-dependent architecture of thalamic reticular subnetworks. *Cell, 158*, 808–821.

Hall, C. C., Zhao, J., & Shafir, E. (2014). Self-affirmation among the poor: Cognitive and behavioral implications. *Psychological Science, 25*(2), 619–625.

Hammack, P. L., & Toolis, E. (2014). Narrative and the social construction of adulthood. *New Directions for Child and Adolescent Development, 2014*(145), 43–56.

Hamre, B. K., & Pianta, R. C. (2001). Early teacher–child relationships and the trajectory of children's school outcomes through eighth grade. *Child Development, 72*(2), 625–638.

Hamre, B. K., & Pianta, R. C. (2005). Can instructional and emotional support in the first-grade classroom make a difference for children at risk of school failure? *Child Development, 76*(5), 949–967.

Hamre, B. K., & Pianta, R. C. (2006). Student-teacher relationships. In G. C. Bear & K. M. Minke (Eds.), *Children's needs III: Development, prevention, and intervention* (pp. 59–71). Washington, DC: National Association of School Psychologists.

Hanson, J. L., Chandra, A., Wolfe, B. L., & Pollak, S. D. (2011). Association between income and the hippocampus. *PLoS ONE, 6*(5), e18712.

Hanushek, E. A. (2005). The economics of school quality. *German Economic Review, 6*(3), 269–286.

Hanushek, E. A. (2011). Valuing teachers: How much is a good teacher worth? *Education Next, 11*(3), 40–45.

Hart, B., & Risley, T. R. (1995). *Meaningful differences in the everyday experiences of young American children.* Baltimore: Brookes.

Hasenstaub, A., Sachdev, R. N., & McCormick, D. A. (2007). State changes rapidly modulate cortical neuronal responsiveness. *Journal of Neuroscience, 27*(36), 9607–9622.

Hattie, J. A. (2009). *Visible learning: A synthesis of over 800 meta-analyses relating to achievement.* New York: Routledge.

Hattie, J. A., & Timperley, H. (2007). The power of feedback. *Review of Educational Research, 77*(1), 81–112.

Haycock, K. (1998). Education Trust report: Good teaching matters . . . a lot. *Education Trust, 3*(2), 2–15.

Heckman, J. J. (2006). Skill formation and the economics of investing in disadvantaged children. *Science, 312*(5782), 1900–1902.

Heller, A. S., van Reekum, C. M., Schaefer, S. M., Lapate, R. C., Radler, B. T., Ryff, C. D., et al. (2013). Sustained striatal activity predicts eudaimonic well-being and cortisol output. *Psychological Science, 24*(11), 2191–2200.

Henderson, W. (2012). *All the world's their stage: Connecting content to students' futures.* Accessed at http://tntp.org/assets/documents/TNTP_FishmanPrizeSeries_2012.pdf on October 22, 2015.

Hofferth, S. L. (1996). Child care in the United States today. *The Future of Children, 6*(2), 41–61.

Hofstetter, S., Tavor, I., Moryosef, S. T., & Assaf, Y. (2013). Short-term learning induces white matter plasticity in the fornix. *The Journal of Neuroscience, 33*(12), 844–850.

Hoy, W. K., Tarter, C. J., & Hoy, A. W. (2006). Academic optimism of schools: A force for student achievement. *American Educational Research Journal, 43*(3), 425–446.

Hughes, J. N., & Kwok, O.-M. (2006). Classroom engagement mediates the effect of teacher–student support on elementary students' peer acceptance: A prospective analysis. *Journal of School Psychology, 43*(6), 465–480.

Hughes, J. N., Luo, W., Kwok, O.-M., & Loyd, L. K. (2008). Teacher–student support, effortful engagement, and achievement: A 3-year longitudinal study. *Journal of Educational Psychology, 100*(1), 1–14.

Immordino-Yang, M. H., & Damasio, A. (2007). We feel, therefore we learn: The relevance of affective and social neuroscience to education. *Mind, Brain, and Education, 1*(1), 3–10.

Irish, J. (2012). *Crush Lusher: Investing students in something bigger than themselves.* Accessed at http://tntp.org/assets/documents/TNTP_FishmanPrizeSeries_2012.pdf on October 22, 2015.

Isen, A. M., Daubman, K. A., & Nowicki, G. P. (1987). Positive affect facilitates creative problem solving. *Journal of Personality and Social Psychology, 52,* 1122–1131.

Iversen, R. R., & Farber, N. B. (1996). Transmission of family values, work, and welfare among poor urban black women. *Work and Occupations, 23*(4), 437–460.

Jackson, J. (1982). *You may not be responsible for being down, but you must be responsible for getting up.* Accessed at www.azquotes.com/quote/765869 on July 25, 2015.

Jackson, R. R. (2011). *How to motivate reluctant learners.* Alexandria, VA: Association for Supervision and Curriculum Development.

Jackson, Y. (2011). *The pedagogy of confidence: Inspiring high intellectual performance in urban schools.* New York: Teachers College Press.

Jacoby, J. M., & Podell, L. (2013). *Mentoring for school success: Creating positive changes.* Newark, NJ: Adolescent Mentoring.

Jaeggi, S. M., Buschkuehl, M., Jonides, J., & Perrig, W. J. (2008). Improving fluid intelligence with training on working memory. *Proceedings of the National Academy of Sciences of the United States of America, 105*(19), 6829–6833.

JayMJ23. (2006). *Michael Jordan "failure" Nike commercial* [YouTube video]. Accessed at www.youtube.com/watch?v=45mMioJ5szc on October 28, 2015.

Jensen, E. (2014). *A descriptive study of differences between teachers at high and low performing Title I elementary schools* (UMI No. 3616282). Santa Barbara, CA: Fielding Graduate University.

Jimerson, S., Egeland, B., Sroufe, L. A., & Carlson, B. (2000). A prospective longitudinal study of high school dropouts: Examining multiple predictors across development. *Journal of School Psychology, 38*(6), 525–549.

Job, V., Walton, G. M., Bernecker, K., & Dweck, C. S. (2015). Implicit theories about willpower predict self-regulation and grades in everyday life. *Journal of Personality and Social Psychology, 108,* 637–647.

Johnson, J. F., Uline, C. L., & Perez, L. G. (2014). The quest for mastery. *Educational Leadership, 72*(2), 48–53.

Kagan, L., Kagan, M., Kagan, S. (1997). *Cooperative learning structures for teambuilding*. San Clement, CA: Kagan Cooperative Learning.

Kaiman, J., Holpuch, A., Smith, D., Watts, J., & Topping, A. (2013, October 18). *Beyond Malala: Six teenagers changing the world*. Accessed at www.theguardian.com/world/2013/oct/18/teenagers-changing-world-malala-yousafzai on October 21, 2015.

Kennedy, J. F. (1962, September). *Address at Rice University on the nation's space effort*. Speech presented at Rice University, Houston, TX.

Keshavan, M. S., Giedd, J., Lau, J. Y., Lewis, D. A., & Paus, T. (2014). Changes in the adolescent brain and the pathophysiology of psychotic disorders. *Lancet Psychiatry, 7*, 549–558

Kim, Y. Y., Choi, J. M., Kim, S. Y., Park, S. K., Lee, S. H., & Lee, K. H. (2002). Changes in EEG of children during brain respiration-training. *American Journal of Chinese Medicine, 30*(2–3), 405–417.

Kimble, M., Boxwala, M., Bean, W., Maletsky, K., Halper, J., Spollen, K., et al. (2014). The impact of hypervigilance: Evidence for a forward feedback loop. *Journal of Anxiety Disorders, 28*(2), 241–245.

Kirsch, I. (Ed.). (1999). *How expectancies shape experience*. Washington, DC: American Psychological Association.

Kluger, A. N., & DeNisi, A. S. (1996). The effects of feedback interventions on performance: A historical review, a meta-analysis, and a preliminary feedback intervention theory. *Psychological Bulletin, 119*(2), 254–284.

Knowles, M., Rabinowich, J., Ettinger de Cuba, S., Cutts, D. B., & Chilton, M. (2015, July). "Do you wanna breathe or eat?": Parent perspectives on child health consequences of food insecurity, trade-offs, and toxic stress. *Maternal and Child Health Journal*, 1–8.

Knudsen, E. I., Heckman, J. J., Cameron, J. L., & Shonkoff, J. P. (2006). Economic, neurobiological, and behavioral perspectives on building America's future workforce. *Proceedings of the National Academy of Sciences of the United States of America, 103*(27), 10155–10162.

Kohl, J. V. (2012). Human pheromones and food odors: Epigenetic influences on the socioaffective nature of evolved behaviors. *Socioaffective Neuroscience and Psychology, 2*, 17338.

Konrath, S. H., O'Brien, E. H., & Hsing, C. (2011). Changes in dispositional empathy in American college students over time: A meta-analysis. *Personality and Social Psychology Review, 15*(2), 180–198.

Kulik, C.-L. C., & Kulik, J. A. (1987). Mastery testing and student learning: A meta-analysis. *Journal of Educational Technology Systems, 15*(3), 325–345.

Ladd, G. W., & Dinella, L. M. (2009). Continuity and change in early school engagement: Predictive of children's achievement trajectories from first to eighth grade? *Journal of Educational Psychology, 101*(1), 190–206.

Lamm, C., Batson, C. D., & Decety, J. (2007). The neural substrate of human empathy: Effects of perspective-taking and cognitive appraisal. *Journal of Cognitive Neuroscience, 19*(1), 42–58.

Landis, D., Gaylord-Harden, N. K., Malinowski, S. L., Grant, K. E., Carleton, R. A., & Ford, R. E. (2007). Urban adolescent stress and hopelessness. *Journal of Adolescence, 30*(6), 1051–1070.

Lee, H., Devlin, J. T., Shakeshaft, C., Stewart, L. H., Brennan, A., Glensman, J., et al. (2007). Anatomical traces of vocabulary acquisition in the adolescent brain. *The Journal of Neuroscience, 27*(5), 1184–1189.

Lee, T. M., Wong, M. L., Lau, B. W., Lee, J. C., Yau, S. Y., So, K. F. (2014). Aerobic exercise interacts with neurotrophic factors to predict cognitive functioning in adolescents. *Psychoneuroendocrinology, 39*, 214–224.

Lenhart, A. (2009). *Teens and sexting: How and why minor teens are sending sexually suggestive nude or nearly nude images via text messaging.* Washington, DC: Pew Internet and American Life Project. Accessed at www.pewinternet.org/files/old-media//Files /Reports/2009/PIP_Teens_and_Sexting.pdf on April 12, 2014.

Lewis, G. J., & Bates, T. C. (2010). Genetic evidence for multiple biological mechanisms underlying in-group favoritism. *Psychological Science, 21*(11), 1623–1628.

Liew, J., Chen, Q., & Hughes, J. N. (2010). Child effortful control, teacher-student relationships, and achievement in academically at-risk children: Additive and interactive effects. *Early Childhood Research Quarterly, 25*(1), 51–64.

Luby, J. L., Barch, D. M., Belden, A., Gaffrey, M. S., Tillman, R., Babb, C., et al. (2012). Maternal support in early childhood predicts larger hippocampal volumes at school age. *Proceedings of the National Academy of Sciences of the United States of America, 109*(8), 2854–2859.

Luby, J. L., Belden, A., Botteron, K., Marrus, N., Harms, M. P., Babb, C., et al. (2013). The effects of poverty on childhood brain development: The mediating effect of caregiving and stressful life events. *Journal of the American Medical Association Pediatrics, 167*(12), 1135–1142.

Lyons, K. (2012). *"You are here": Inspiring curiosity by making content personal.* Accessed at http://tntp.org/assets/documents/TNTP_FishmanPrizeSeries_2012.pdf on October 22, 2015.

Lysakowski, R. S., & Walberg, H. J. (1982). Instructional effects of cues, participation, and corrective feedback: A quantitative synthesis. *American Educational Research Journal, 19*(4), 559–578.

Lyubomirsky, S., King, L., & Diener, E. (2005). The benefits of frequent positive affect: Does happiness lead to success? *Psychological Bulletin, 131*(6), 803–855.

Mackey, A. P., Singley, A. T. M., Wendelken, C., & Bunge, S. A. (2015). Characterizing behavioral and brain changes associated with practicing reasoning skills. *PLoS ONE, 10*(9).

Macnamara, B. N., Hambrick, D. Z., & Oswald, F. L. (2014). Deliberate practice and performance in music, games, sports, education, and professions: A meta-analysis. *Psychological Science, 25*(8), 1608–1618.

Mahar, M. T., Murphy, S. K., Rowe, D. A., Golden, J., Shields, A. T., & Raedeke, T. D. (2006). Effects of a classroom-based program on physical activity and on-task behavior. *Medicine and Science in Sports and Exercise, 38*(12), 2086–2094.

Maldonado-Carreño, C., & Votruba-Drzal, E. (2011). Teacher-child relationships and the development of academic and behavioral skills during elementary school: A within- and between-child analysis. *Child Development, 82*(2), 601–616.

Mangels, J. A., Good, C., Whiteman, R. C., Maniscalco, B., & Dweck, C. S. (2012). Emotion blocks the path to learning under stereotype threat. *Social Cognitive and Affective Neuroscience, 7*(2), 230–241.

Mangen, A., & Velay, J.-L. (2010). Digitizing literacy: Reflections on the haptics of writing. In M. H. Zadeh (Ed.), *Advances in haptics*. Rijeka, Croatia: InTech. Accessed at www.intechopen.com/books/advances-in-haptics/digitizing-literacy-reflections-on-the-haptics-of-writing on April 25, 2014.

Mani, A., Mullainathan, S., Shafir, E., & Zhao, J. (2013). Poverty impedes cognitive function. *Science, 341*(6149), 976–980.

Marks, H. M. (2000). Student engagement in instructional activity: Patterns in the elementary, middle, and high school years. *American Educational Research Journal, 37*(1), 153–184.

Marzano, R. J. (1998). *A theory-based meta-analysis of research on instruction*. Aurora, CO: Mid-continent Regional Educational Laboratory. Accessed at www.peecworks.org/peec/peec_research/I01795EFA.2/Marzano%20Instruction%20Meta_An.pdf on March 22, 2015.

Marzano, R. J. (2003). *Classroom management that works: Research-based strategies for every teacher*. Alexandria, VA: Association for Supervision and Curriculum Development.

Marzano, R. J., & Pickering, D. J. (2011). *The highly engaged classroom*. Bloomington, IN: Marzano Research.

Marzano, R. J., Pickering, D. J., & Pollock, J. E. (2001). *Classroom instruction that works: Research-based strategies for increasing student achievement*. Alexandria, VA: Association for Supervision and Curriculum Development.

Maxwell, L. A. (2014). U.S. school enrollment hits majority-minority milestone. *Education Week*. Accessed at www.edweek.org/ew/articles/2014/08/20/01demographics.h34.html on October 23, 2015.

May, A., Hajak, G., Gänssbauer, S., Steffens, T., Langguth, B., Kleinjung, T., et al. (2007). Structural brain alterations following 5 days of intervention: Dynamic aspects of neuroplasticity. *Cerebral Cortex: Oxford Journals, 17*(1), 205–210.

McEwen, B. S. (2000). The neurobiology of stress: From serendipity to clinical relevance. *Brain Research Interactive, 886*(2000), 172–189.

McEwen, B. S. (2002). *The end of stress as we know it*. New York: Dana Press.

McEwen, B. S. (2008). Central effects of stress hormones in health and disease: Understanding the protective and damaging effects of stress and stress mediators. *European Journal of Pharmacology, 583*(2–3), 174–185.

McGonigal, K. (2012). *The willpower instinct: How self-control works, why it matters, and what you can do to get more of it.* New York: Avery.

McGuigan, L., & Hoy, W. K. (2006). Principal leadership: Creating a culture of academic optimism to improve achievement for all students. *Leadership and Policy in Schools, 5*(3), 203–229.

McLanahan, S. S. (1999). Parent absence or poverty: Which matters more? In G. Duncan & J. Brooks-Gunn, J. (Eds.), *Consequences of growing up poor* (pp. 35–48). New York: Russell Sage Foundation.

McLoyd, V. C. (1988). Socioeconomic disadvantage and child development. *American Psychologist, 53*(2), 185–204.

McNamara, T. P. (2005). *Semantic priming: Perspectives from memory and word recognition.* New York: Psychology Press.

McTighe, J., & Wiggins, G. (2013). *Essential questions: Opening doors to student understanding.* Alexandria, VA: Association for Supervision and Curriculum Development.

Mehrabian, A. (2000). Beyond IQ: Broad-based measurement of individual success potential or "emotional intelligence." *Genetic, Social, and General Psychology Monographs, 126*(2), 133–239.

Miller, S. L., & Maner, J. K. (2010). Scent of a woman: Men's testosterone responses to olfactory ovulation cues. *Psychological Science, 21*(2), 276–283.

Miller-Lewis, L. R., Sawyer, A. C., Searle, A. K., Mittinty, M. N., Sawyer, M. G., & Lynch, J. W. (2014). Student-teacher relationship trajectories and mental health problems in young children. *BMC Psychology, 12*, 27.

Molenberghs, P., Cunnington, R., & Mattingley, J. B. (2009). Is the mirror neuron system involved in imitation?: A short review and meta-analysis. *Neuroscience and Biobehavioral Reviews, 33*(7), 975–980.

Moriceau, S., & Sullivan, R. M. (2005). Neurobiology of infant attachment. *Developmental Psychobiology, 47*(3), 230–242.

National Center for Health Statistics. (2008). Births, marriages, divorces, and deaths: Provisional data for 2007. *National Vital Statistics Reports, 56*(21). Accessed at www.cdc.gov/nchs/data/nvsr/nvsr56/nvsr56_21.pdf on May 22, 2015.

Nayar, D. (Producer), & Chadha, G. (Producer and Director). (2003). *Bend it like Beckham* [Motion picture]. United States: 20th Century Fox Home Entertainment.

Noble, K. G., Norman, M. F., & Farah, M. J. (2005). Neurocognitive correlates of socioeconomic status in kindergarten children. *Developmental Science, 8*(1), 74–87.

Noble, K. G., Wolmetz, M. E., Ochs, L. G., Farah, M. J., & McCandliss, B. D. (2006). Brain-behavior relationships in reading acquisition are modulated by socioeconomic factors. *Developmental Science, 9*(6), 642–654.

Noggle, J. J., Steiner, N. J., Minami, T., & Khalsa, S. B. S. (2012). Benefits of yoga for psychosocial well-being in a US high school curriculum: A preliminary randomized controlled trial. *Journal of Developmental and Behavioral Pediatrics, 33*(3), 193–201.

O'Keefe, P. A., & Linnenbrink-Garcia, L. (2014). The role of interest in optimizing performance and self-regulation. *Journal of Experimental Social Psychology*, *53*, 70–78.

Olejnik, S., & Algina, J. (2000). Measures of effect size for comparative studies: Applications, interpretations, and limitations. *Contemporary Educational Psychology*, *25*(3), 241–286.

Oppezzo, M., & Schwartz, D. L. (2014). Give your ideas some legs: The positive effect of walking on creative thinking. *Journal of Experimental Psychology: Learning, Memory, and Cognition*, *40*(4), 1142–1152.

Palincsar, A. S., & Brown, A. L. (1984). Reciprocal teaching of comprehension-fostering and comprehension-monitoring activities. *Cognition and Instruction*, *1*(2), 117–175.

Passolunghi, M. C., Mammarella, I. C., & Altoe, G. (2008). Cognitive abilities as precursors of the early acquisition of mathematical skills during first through second grades. *Developmental Neuropsychology*, *33*(3), 229–250.

Peterson, C., Maier, S. F., & Seligman, M. E. (1995). *Learned helplessness.* London: Oxford University Press.

Petty, G. (2006). *Evidence-based teaching: A practical approach.* Cheltenham, United Kingdom: Nelson Thornes.

Petty, G. (2009). *Evidence-based teaching.* Cheltenham, United Kingdom: Nelson Thornes.

Pfeffer, F. T., & Hällsten, M. (2012). *Mobility regimes and parental wealth: The United States, Germany, and Sweden in comparison.* (PSC Research Report No. 12-766). Accessed at www.psc.isr.umich.edu/pubs/pdf/rr12-766.pdf on October 14, 2015.

Phinney, J. S., Lochner, B. T., & Murphy, R. (1990). Ethnic identity development and psychological adjustment in adolescence. In A. R. Stiffman & L. E. Davis (Eds.), *Ethnic issues in adolescent mental health* (pp. 53–72). Newbury Park, CA: SAGE.

Pianta, R. C., Belsky, J., Houts, R., & Morrison, F. (2007). Opportunities to learn in America's elementary classrooms. *Science*, *315*(5820), 1795–1796.

Pianta, R. C., Hamre, B. K., & Allen, J. P. (2012). Teacher-student relationships and engagement: Conceptualizing, measuring, and improving the capacity of classroom interactions. In S. L. Christenson, A. L. Reschly, & C. Wylie (Eds.), *Handbook of research on student engagement* (pp. 365–386). New York: Springer Media.

Pink, D. H. (2009). *Drive: The surprising truth about what motivates us.* New York: Riverhead Books.

Polikoff, M. S., McEachin, A. J., Wrabel, S. L., & Duque, M. (2013). The waive of the future?: School accountability in the waiver era. *Educational Researcher*, *43*(1), 45–54.

Pungello, E. P., Kainz, K., Burchinal, M., Wasik, B. H., Sparling, J. J., Ramey, C. T., et al. (2010). Early educational intervention, early cumulative risk, and the early home environment as predictors of young adult outcomes within a high-risk sample. *Child Development*, *81*(1), 410–426.

Quintana, S. M. (2007). Racial and ethnic identity: Developmental perspectives and research. *Journal of Counseling Psychology*, *54*(3), 259–270.

Raichle, M. E., MacLeod, A. M., Snyder, A. Z., Powers, W. J., Gusnard, D. A., & Shulman, G. L. (2001). A default mode of brain function. *Proceedings of the National Academy of Sciences of the United States of America*, *98*(2), 676–682.

Ramirez, G., & Beilock, S. L. (2011). Writing about testing worries boosts exam performance in the classroom. *Science*, *331*(6014), 211–213.

Rand, K. L. (2009). Hope and optimism: Latent structures and influences on grade expectancy and academic performance. *Journal of Personality*, *77*(1), 231–260.

Rattan, A., Good, C., & Dweck, C. S. (2012). "It's ok—Not everyone can be good at math": Instructors with an entity theory comfort (and demotivate) students. *Journal of Experimental Social Psychology*, *48*(3), 731–737.

Rector, R. (2012). *Marriage: America's greatest weapon against child poverty*. Washington, DC: U.S. Bureau of the Census. Accessed at http://factfinder2.census.gov/faces /tableservices/jsf/pages/productview.xhtml?pid=ACS_09_3YR_S1702&prodType=table on October 14, 2015.

Reis, S., Colbert, R., & Hébert, T. (2005). Understanding resilience in diverse, talented students in an urban high school. *Roeper Review*, *27*(2), 110–120.

Reyes, M. R., Brackett, M. A., Rivers, S. E., White, M., & Salovey, P. (2012). Classroom emotional climate, student engagement, and academic achievement. *Journal of Educational Psychology*, *104*(3), 700–712.

Riedl, K., Jensen, K., Call, J., & Tomasello, M. (2015). Restorative justice in children. *Current Biology*, *25*(13), 1731–1735.

Rivkin, S. G., Hanushek, E. A., & Kain, J. F. (2005). Teachers, schools, and academic achievement. *Econometrica*, *73*(2), 417–458.

Robertson-Kraft, C., & Duckworth, A. L. (2014). True grit: Trait-level perseverance and passion for long-term goals predicts effectiveness and retention among novice teachers. *Teachers College Record*, *116*(3), 1–27.

Robinson, K. (2013). *Gettin' Messi: How mistakes make mathematicians*. Accessed at http:// tntp.org/assets/documents/TNTP_FishmanPrizeSeries_2013.pdf on November 10, 2015.

Rockoff, J. E. (2004). The impact of individual teachers on student achievement: Evidence from panel data. *American Economic Review*, *94*(2), 247–252.

Roorda, D. L., Koomen, H. M. Y., Spilt, J. L., & Oort, F. J. (2011). The influence of affective teacher–student relationships on students' school engagement and achievement: A meta-analytic approach. *Review of Educational Research*, *81*(4), 493–529.

Rosenfeld, L. R., Richman, J. M., & Bowen, G. L. (1998). Low social support among at-risk adolescents. *Social Work in Education*, *20*(4), 245–260.

Rosenshine, B., & Meister, C. (1994). Reciprocal teaching: A review of the research. *Review of Educational Research*, *64*(4), 479–530.

Rosenthal, R., & Jacobson, L. (1966). Teachers' expectancies: Determinants of pupils' IQ gains. *Psychological Reports*, *19*(1), 115–118.

Rosenthal, R., & Jacobson, L. (1992). *Pygmalion in the classroom: Teacher expectation and pupils' intellectual development* (Expanded ed.). New York: Irvington.

Ross, L. (2012). *Here we grow again: Building a winning team in the classroom.* Accessed at http://tntp.org/assets/documents/TNTP_FishmanPrizeSeries_2012.pdf on October 22, 2015.

Rowe, G., Hirsh, J. B., & Anderson, A. K. (2007). Positive affect increases the breadth of attentional selection. *Proceedings of the National Academy of Sciences of the United States of America, 104*(1), 383–388.

Rumberger, R. (2004). Why students drop out of school. In G. Orfield (Ed.), *Dropouts in America: Confronting the graduation rate crisis* (pp. 131–155). Cambridge, MA: Harvard Education Press.

Sanders, W. L., & Horn, S. P. (1998). Research findings from the Tennessee value-added assessment system (TVAAS) database: Implications for educational evaluation and research. *Journal of Personnel Evaluation in Education, 12*(3), 247–256.

Santiago, C. D., Etter, E. M., Wadsworth, M. E., & Raviv, T. (2012). Predictors of responses to stress among families coping with poverty-related stress. *Anxiety, Stress, and Coping, 25*(3), 239–258.

Schumann, K., Zaki, J., & Dweck, C. S. (2014). Addressing the empathy deficit: Beliefs about the malleability of empathy predict effortful responses when empathy is challenging. *Journal of Personality and Social Psychology, 107*(3), 475–493.

Schwenninger, S. R., & Sherraden, S. (2011, April). *The American middle class under stress.* Washington, DC: New America Foundation. Accessed at http://garysmettler.com /wp-content/uploads/2014/09/The-American-Middle-Class-Under-Stress-2011.pdf on May 22, 2015.

Seastrom, M., Hoffman, L., Chapman, C., & Stillwell, R. (2005, October). *The averaged freshman graduation rate for public high schools from the Common Core of data: School years 2001–02 and 2002–03* (NCES 2006–601). Washington, DC: National Center for Education Statistics. Accessed at http://nces.ed.gov/pubs2006/2006601.pdf on April 1, 2012.

Sellers, R. M., Caldwell, C. H., Schmeelk-Cone, K. H., & Zimmerman, M. A. (2003). Racial identity, racial discrimination, perceived stress, and psychological distress among African American young adults. *Journal of Health and Social Behavior, 44*(3), 302–317.

Serrano, M. A., Moya-Albiol, L., & Salvador, A. (2014). Endocrine and mood responses to two working days in female teachers. *Spanish Journal of Psychology, 17*(e25), 1–11.

Shaefer, H. L., & Edin, K. (2012, February). *Extreme poverty in the United States, 1996 to 2011* [Policy brief]. Ann Arbor, MI: National Poverty Center. Accessed at www.npc .umich.edu/publications/policy_briefs/brief28/policybrief28.pdf on May 22, 2015.

Shah, A. K., Mullainathan, S., & Shafir, E. (2012). Some consequences of having too little. *Science, 338*(6107), 682–685.

Shaw, G. B. (1903). *Man and Superman: A comedy and a philosophy.* New York: Brentano's.

Shernoff, D. J., Csikszentmihalyi, M., Schneider, B., & Shernoff, E. S. (2003). Student engagement in high school classrooms from the perspective of flow theory. *School Psychology Quarterly, 18*(2), 158–176.

Sheynikhovich, D., Otani, S., & Arleo, A. (2013). Dopaminergic control of long-term depression/long-term potentiation threshold in prefrontal cortex. *Journal of Neuroscience, 33*(34), 13914–13926.

Sinek, S. (2009). *Start with why: How great leaders inspire everyone to take action.* New York: Portfolio.

Slepian, M. L., & Ambady, N. (2012). Fluid movement and creativity. *Journal of Experimental Psychology: General, 141*(4), 625–629.

Smiley, P. A., & Dweck, C. S. (1994). Individual differences in achievement goals among young children. *Child Development, 65*(6), 1723–1743.

Song, X., Wang, H., Zheng, L., Chen, D., & Wang, Z. (2010). The relationship between problem behavior and neurotransmitter deficiency in adolescents. *Journal of Huazhong University of Science and Technology (Medical Sciences), 30*(6), 714–719.

Stipek, D. (2002). Good instruction is motivating. In A. Wigfield & J. S. Eccles (Eds.), *Development of achievement motivation* (pp. 309–332). San Diego, CA: Academic Press.

Steiger, S., Haberer, W., & Müller, J. K. (2011). Social environment determines degree of chemical signalling. *Biology Letters, 7*(6), 822–824.

Stewart, L., Henson, R., Kampe, K., Walsh, V., Turner, R., & Frith, U. (2003). Brain changes after learning to read and play music. *Neuroimage, 20*(1), 71–83.

Suitts, S. (2015). *A new majority: Low income students now a majority in the nation's public schools* (Research bulletin). Atlanta, GA: Southern Education Foundation. Accessed at www.southerneducation.org/Our-Strategies/Research-and-Publications/New-Majority -Diverse-Majority-Report-Series/A-New-Majority-2015-Update-Low-Income-Students -Now on May 22, 2015.

Sutoo, D., & Akiyama, K. (2003). Regulation of brain function by exercise. *Neurobiology of Disease, 13*(1), 1–14.

Tanner, M. (2014). *War on poverty at 50: Despite trillions spent, poverty won.* Washington, DC: Cato Institute. Accessed at www.cato.org/publications/commentary/war-poverty -50-despite-trillions-spent-poverty-won on October 14, 2014.

Temple, E., Deutsch, G. K., Poldrack, R. A., Miller, S. L., Tallal, P., Merzenich, M. M., et al. (2003). Neural deficits in children with dyslexia ameliorated by behavioral remediation: Evidence from functional MRI. *Proceedings of the National Academy of Sciences of the United States of America, 100*(5), 2860–2865.

Terjestam, Y., Jouper, J., & Johansson, C. (2010). Effects of scheduled qigong exercise on pupils' well-being, self-image, distress, and stress. *Journal of Alternative and Complementary Medicine, 16*(9), 939–944.

Tine, M. (2014). Working memory differences between children living in rural and urban poverty. *Journal of Cognition and Development, 15*(4), 599–613.

Todd, R. M., & Anderson, A. K. (2009). Six degrees of separation: The amygdala regulates social behavior and perception. *Nature Neuroscience, 12*, 1217–1218.

Tomporowski, P. D., Davis, C. L., Miller, P. H., & Naglieri, J. A. (2008). Exercise and children's intelligence, cognition, and academic achievement. *Educational Psychology Review, 20*(2), 111–131.

Tough, P. (2012). *How children succeed: Grit, curiosity, and the hidden power of character.* New York: Houghton Mifflin Harcourt.

University of Pennsylvania School of Arts and Sciences. (2011). *12-item grit scale.* Accessed at www.sas.upenn.edu/~duckwort/images/12-item%20Grit%20Scale.05312011.pdf on May 22, 2015.

U.S. Census Bureau. (n.d.a). *American FactFinder: Community facts.* Accessed at http://factfinder2.census.gov/faces/nav/jsf/pages/community_facts.xhtml on May 22, 2015.

U.S. Census Bureau. (n.d.b). *Historical poverty tables—people: Table 2. Poverty status, by family relationship, race, and Hispanic origin.* Accessed at www.census.gov/hhes/www/poverty/data/historical/people.html on May 22, 2015.

U.S. Census Bureau. (2010). *American FactFinder: Poverty status in the past 12 months of families (2010 American Community Survey 1-year estimates).* Accessed at http://factfinder2.census.gov/faces/tableservices/jsf/pages/productview.xhtml?pid=ACS_10_1YR_S1702&prodType=table on April 10, 2012.

U.S. Department of Agriculture, Food and Nutrition Service. (2013). *National School Lunch Program.* Accessed at www.fns.usda.gov/sites/default/files/NSLPFactSheet.pdf on October 14, 2015.

U.S. Department of Agriculture, Office of Inspector General. (2013). *Overlap and duplication in Food and Nutrition Service's nutrition programs* (Audit Report No. 27001–0001–10). Washington, DC: Author. Accessed at www.usda.gov/oig/webdocs/27001-0001-10.pdf on May 22, 2015.

U.S. Department of Education Office for Civil Rights. (2014). *Civil rights data collection: Data snapshot: School discipline.* Accessed at http://ocrdata.ed.gov/Downloads/CRDC-School-Discipline-Snapshot.pdf on October 14, 2015.

U.S. Department of the Treasury. (2007). *Income mobility in the U.S. from 1996 to 2005.* Washington, DC: Author. Accessed at www.treasury.gov/resource-center/tax-policy/Documents/incomemobilitystudy03-08revise.pdf on May 22, 2015.

Valentine, J. (2005). *Statistical differences for the percentages of student engagement as measured by IPI categories between very successful and very unsuccessful middle schools.* Columbia, MO: Middle Level Leadership Center.

Valentine, J., & Collins, J. (2011, April 11). *Student engagement and achievement on high-stakes tests: A HLM analysis across 68 middle schools.* Presented at the American Educational Research Association annual conference in New Orleans, LA.

Wanless, S. B., McClelland, M. M., Acock, A. C., Chen, F.-M., & Chen, J.-L. (2011). Behavioral regulation and early academic achievement in Taiwan. *Early Education and Development, 22*(1), 1–28.

Wanless, S. B., McClelland, M. M., Tominey, S. L., & Acock, A. C. (2011). The influence of demographic risk factors on children's behavioral regulation in prekindergarten and kindergarten. *Early Education and Development, 22*(3), 461–488.

Wenglinsky, H. (2000). *How teaching matters: Bringing the classroom back into discussions of teacher quality.* Princeton, NJ: Educational Testing Service.

Wenglinsky, H. (2002). How schools matter: The link between teacher classroom practices and student academic performance. *Education Policy Analysis Archives, 10*(12). Accessed at http://epaa.asu.edu/ojs/article/download/291/417 on May 22, 2015.

Wentzel, K. R. (1997). Student motivation in middle school: The role of perceived pedagogical caring. *Journal of Educational Psychology, 89*(3), 411–419.

Wiliam, D., & Thompson, M. (2007). Integrating assessment with instruction: What will it take to make it work? In C. A. Dwyer (Ed.), *The future of assessment: Shaping teaching and learning* (pp. 53–82). Mahwah, NJ: Erlbaum.

Williams, J. H. G., Perrett, D. I., Waiter, G. D., & Pechey, S. (2007). Differential effects of tryptophan depletion on emotion processing according to face direction. *Social Cognitive and Affective Neuroscience, 2*(4), 264–273.

Willett, J. B., Yamashita, J. J. M., & Anderson, R. D. (1983). A meta-analysis of instructional systems applied in science teaching. *Journal of Research in Science Teaching, 20*(5), 405–417.

Wilson, T. D. (2011). *Redirect: The surprising new science of psychological change.* New York: Little, Brown.

Wilson, W. J. (1997). *When work disappears: The world of the new urban poor.* New York: Knopf.

Winerman, L. (2013). What sets high achievers apart? *Monitor on Psychology, 44*(11), 28–31.

Wu, M., Morgan, K., Hur, J., Schifrin, K., Gordon, L., Russell, G., et al. (2012). *The irreplaceables: Understanding the real retention crisis in America's urban schools.* Brooklyn, NY: New Teacher Project. Accessed at www.tntp.org/assets/documents/TNTP_Irreplaceables_2012.pdf on March 5, 2013.

Yazzie-Mintz, E. (2007a). *National high school student engagement survey by IU reveals unengaged students* [Press release]. Bloomington: Indiana University. Accessed at www.indiana.edu/~soenews/news/news1172622996.html on April 12, 2012.

Yazzie-Mintz, E. (2007b). *Voices of students on engagement: A report of the 2006 High School Survey of Student Engagement.* Bloomington, IN: Center for Evaluation and Education Policy. Accessed at http://ceep.indiana.edu/hssse/images/HSSSE%20Overview%20Report%20-%202006.pdf on May 22, 2015.

Yeager, D. S., Henderson, M. D., Paunesku, D., Walton, G. M., D'Mello, S., Spitzer, B. J., et al. (2014). Boring but important: A self-transcendent purpose for learning fosters academic self-regulation. *Journal of Personality and Social Psychology, 107*(4), 559–580.

Zink, C. F., Tong, Y., Chen, Q., Bassett, D. S., Stein, J. L., & Meyer-Lindenberg, A. (2008). Know your place: Neural processing of social hierarchy in humans. *Neuron, 58*(2), 273–283.

Index

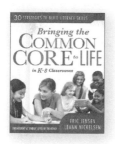

Bringing the Common Core to Life in K–8 Classrooms
Eric Jensen and LeAnn Nickelsen
Discover strategies to promote student mastery of the
Common Core State Standards for English language arts across
the curriculum. Develop the know-how to activate students'
background knowledge to prepare them for learning and
effectively structure teaching to empower all students.
BKF442

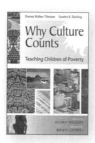

Why Culture Counts
Donna Walker Tileston and Sandra K. Darling
Learn a four-step research-based program for differentiating
instruction based on the cultural needs, beliefs, and values
of diverse learners. The authors show you how to build
teacher background knowledge; plan for differentiation; and
differentiate context, content, process, product, and assessment.
BKF255

Overcoming the Achievement Gap Trap
Anthony Muhammad
Ensure learning equality in every classroom. Investigate previous
and current policies designed to help close the achievement
gap. Explore strategies for adopting a new mindset that frees
educators and students from negative academic performance
expectations.
BKF618

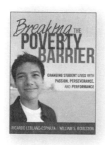

Breaking the Poverty Barrier
Ricardo LeBlanc-Esparza and William S. Roulston
Strong leadership, parent involvement, mentoring, data-based
intervention, and high expectations are known factors in
student success. This book illustrates the specific strategies and
critical steps that transformed a school with shockingly low
proficiency into a National Showcase School.
BKF476

Solution Tree | Press

a division of
Solution Tree

Visit solution-tree.com or call 800.733.6786 to order.

Wait! Your professional development journey doesn't have to end with the last pages of this book.

We realize improving student learning doesn't happen overnight. And your school or district shouldn't be left to puzzle out all the details of this process alone.

No matter where you are on the journey, we're committed to helping you get to the next stage.

Take advantage of everything from **custom workshops** to **keynote presentations** and **interactive web and video conferencing**. We can even help you develop an action plan tailored to fit your specific needs.

Let's get the conversation started.

Call 888.763.9045 today.

solution-tree.com